Boredom is Anti-Life: 250 Anecdotes and Stories

David Bruce

Published by David Bruce, 2022.

While every precaution has been taken in the preparation of this book, the publisher assumes no responsibility for errors or omissions, or for damages resulting from the use of the information contained herein.

BOREDOM IS ANTI-LIFE: 250 ANECDOTES AND STORIES

First edition. October 6, 2022.

Copyright © 2022 David Bruce.

ISBN: 979-8215956298

Written by David Bruce.

Table of Contents

Dedication

Dedicated to Carl Eugene Bruce and Josephine Saturday Bruce

My father, Carl Eugene Bruce, died on 24 October 2013. He used to work for Ohio Power, and at one time, his job was to shut off the electricity of people who had not paid their bills. He sometimes would find a home with an impoverished mother and some children. Instead of shutting off their electricity, he would tell the mother that she needed to pay her bill or soon her electricity would be shut off. He would write on a form that no one was home when he stopped by because if no one was home he did not have to shut off their electricity.

The best good deed that anyone ever did for my father occurred after a storm that knocked down many power lines. He and other linemen worked long hours and got wet and cold. Their feet were freezing because water got into their boots and soaked their socks. Fortunately, a kind woman gave my father and the other linemen dry socks to wear.

My mother, Josephine Saturday Bruce, died on 14 June 2003. She used to work at a store that sold clothing. One day, an impoverished mother with a baby clothed in rags walked into the store and started shoplifting in an interesting way: The mother took the rags off her baby and dressed the infant in new clothing. My mother knew that this mother could not afford to buy the clothing, but she helped the mother dress her baby and then she watched as the mother walked out of the store without paying.

***

The doing of good deeds is important. As a free person, you can choose to live your life as a good person or as a bad person. To be a good person, do good deeds. To be a bad person, do bad deeds. If you do good deeds, you will become good. If you do bad deeds, you will become bad. To become the person you want to be, act as if you already are that kind of person. Each of us chooses what kind of person we will become. To become a good person, do the things a good person does. To become a bad person, do the things a bad person does. The opportunity to take action to become the kind of person you want to be is yours.

Human beings have free will. According to the Babylonian Niddah 16b, whenever a baby is to be conceived, the Lailah (angel in charge of contraception) takes the drop of semen that will result in the conception and asks God, "Sovereign of the Universe, what is going to be the fate of this drop? Will it develop into a robust or into a weak person? An intelligent or a stupid person? A wealthy or a poor person?" The Lailah asks all these questions, but it does not ask, "Will it develop into a righteous or a wicked person?" The answer to that question lies in the decisions to be freely made by the human being that is the result of the conception.

A Buddhist monk visiting a class wrote this on the chalkboard: "EVERYONE WANTS TO SAVE THE WORLD, BUT NO ONE WANTS TO HELP MOM DO THE DISHES." The students laughed, but the monk then said, "Statistically, it's highly unlikely that any of you will ever have the opportunity to run into a burning orphanage and rescue an infant. But, in the smallest gesture of kindness — a warm smile, holding the door for the person behind you, shoveling the driveway of the elderly person next door — you have committed an act of immeasurable profundity, because to each of us, our life is our universe."

In her book titled *I Have Chosen to Stay and Fight*, comedian Margaret Cho writes, "I believe that we get complimentary snack-size portions of the afterlife, and we all receive them in a different way." For Ms. Cho, many of her snack-size portions of the afterlife come in hip hop music. Other people get different snack-size portions of the afterlife, and we all must be on the lookout for them when they come our way. And perhaps doing good deeds and experiencing good deeds are snack-size portions of the afterlife.

The Zen master Gisan was taking a bath. The water was too hot, so he asked a student to add some cold water to the bath. The student brought a bucket of cold water, added some cold water to the bath, and then threw the rest of the water on a rocky path. Gisan scolded the student: "Everything can be used. Why did you waste the rest of the water by pouring it on the path? There are some plants nearby which could have used the water. What right do you have to waste even a drop of water?" The student became enlightened and changed his name to Tekisui, which means "Drop of Water."

Front Cover Photograph for *Boredom is Anti-Life: 250 Anecdotes and Stories*:

https://pixabay.com/photos/cornflower-flower-meadow-blue-5427048/

***

Educate Yourself
Read Like A Wolf Eats
Be Excellent to Each Other
Books Then, Books Now, Books Forever

***

Do you know a language other than English? If you do, I give you permission to translate this book, copyright your translation, publish or self-publish it, and keep all the royalties for yourself. (Do give me credit, of course, for the original book.)

Chapter 1: From Actors and Acting to Clothing

Actors and Acting

• Actors often know their own limitations. Early in his career, E.A. Southern tried to act the roles of tragic heroes but discovered that he was not very good at them and so performed other kinds of roles on the stage. He once told theatrical critic John Rankin Towse about a conversation that he had had with fellow actor Edwin Booth: "We were talking, among other things, of Will Stewart, the old dramatic critic, and his capacity for apt and cutting definition. By way of illustration I quoted his remark about my Claude Melnotte, that it 'exhibited all the qualities of a poker except its warmth.'" Mr. Southern then added, "I suppose that my performance was about as bad as anything ever seen upon the stage." Mr. Booth chuckled and then asked, "You never saw my Romeo, did you?"[1]

• Early in his acting career, Sheldon Leonard competed for parts with Sam Levene because they played similar characters. In a road production of *Three Men on a Horse*, Mr. Leonard played a comedic part that Mr. Levene had originated on Broadway. During a dress rehearsal, Mr. Levene stopped by — not to watch Mr. Leonard, but to time his laughs to see if Mr. Leonard was getting bigger laughs than he had gotten. After an especially long laugh, Mr. Levene turned to Mr. Leonard's wife, who was also standing in the back of the theater, and snarled, "What did he do? Drop his pants?"[2]

• When British actor Hugh O'Brian was visiting in New York City and feeling prosperous and famous, a woman said to him, "Excuse me, but would you be kind enough to tell me your name?" Mr. O'Brian also felt mischievous, so he replied, "Certainly, madam, my name's Natalie Wood." The woman turned to her companion and said, "There you are — I told you I was right."[3]

• Filmmaker John Waters once received a resume from a 16-year-old boy whose only acting experience was playing the Easter Bunny in a grade-school play. He offered the boy an acting job, but the boy's parents vetoed his acting career.[4]

Advertising

• In April 2012, the Coca-Cola Company put a special Coke machine in Singapore. It looked like a regular Coke machine, but it had the words "Hug Me" written on it in large letters. Anyone who hugged the machine got a reward: a free cold Coca-Cola. Leonardo O'Grady, ASEAN IMC Director, The Coca-Cola Company, said, "Happiness is contagious. The Coca-Cola Hug Machine is a simple idea to spread some happiness. Our strategy is to deliver doses of happiness in an unexpected, innovative way to engage not only the people present, but the audience at large. Whether you were hugging the machine or experiencing the event online, our goal was the same — to put a smile on your face and share that emotional connection. Reactions were amazing ... people really had fun with it and at one point we had four to five people hugging the machine at the same time as well as each other! In fact, there was a long line of people looking to give hugs — it was really heartwarming." Of course, this is good advertising. Louise Kuegler, Regional Business Director at Ogilvy & Mather Asia Pacific, said, "We're excited to work with The Coca-Cola Company in delivering what is really a very simple idea. All you need to do is give the Coca-Cola Hug Machine a hug and it will love you back, by giving you a free Coke. Something simple and engaging, that lifts people's spirits and brings a smile to their face."[5]

• Magician Herrmann the Great had a knack for publicity. Once, in full view of two police officers, he clumsily picked a handkerchief from the pocket of one of two men. The police officers immediately intervened, and the second man looked in his pockets and discovered that his watch was missing. The police officers asked Herrmann the Great if he had the watch, but he replied that they should look in their pockets. They did, and they discovered both the watch and the handkerchief. By this time, the two men had recognized Herrmann the Great, and they thought the joke was funny. However, the police officers were not amused, and they took the magician to the police station, where they lectured him about respecting the dignity of the police. Of course, the whole affair was written up in the newspapers — exactly as Herrmann the Great had wanted.[6]

• Stan Freberg once parodied soap operas with a skit titled "John and Marsha." The skit consisted only of the words "John" and "Marsha." Marsha would say, "John." John would then say "Marsha." As they said the words, they went through all of the emotions seen on soap operas — love, passion, anger, etc. To advertise the skit, which appeared on a comedy album, Capitol Records printed bumper stickers. Restaurant owners took the bumper stickers, cut them in half, and put "John" on the door to the men's restroom and "Marsha" on the door to the women's restroom. By the way, one of Mr. Freberg's advertisements claimed, "Nine out of ten doctors recommend Chun King chow mein." The advertisement showed ten doctors, nine of whom were Oriental.[7]

Alcohol

• Financial writer Andrew Tobias is often frugal. For example, he buys cheap vodka, and then pours it into bottles bearing the label of an expensive brand. According to Mr. Tobias, "When it comes to mixed drinks, vodka is vodka." By the way, Mr. Tobias knew Bill Clinton before he became President. As a joke, Mr. Tobias once tapped Mr. Clinton on the shoulder and asked, "Now, Bill, forgive me — but *where* is Arkansas again?" Mr. Clinton didn't laugh.[8]

• Noël Coward had just finished having a drink with a VIP when a newspaper reporter spotted him. The reporter asked, "Was it just a friendly drink?" Mr. Coward replied, "My dear boy, have you ever heard of people taking unfriendly drinks?" By the way, Mr. Coward once wrote a letter to Lawrence of Arabia — Aircraftsman T.E. Shaw,

No. 338171. Mr. Coward began the letter, "Dear 338171, May I call you 338?"[9]

• Filmmaker John Waters once went to the supermarket to buy water, an act that seemed suspicious to a lower-class woman, who wondered why on earth anyone would *buy* water. She asked Mr. Waters, "What is that sh*t anyway?" He replied, "Perrier. It's good for hangovers." Hearing that, she smiled, revealing a toothless mouth, and said, "I'll have to get me some."[10]

Art

• Students at MIT have occasionally hacked (that is, pranked) the school's works of art. Actually, one hack really wasn't a hack — it really was a work of art. Artist Scott Raphael Schiamberg installed what appeared to be a field of wheat in Lobby 7. On a Monday in May 1996, students and faculty strolled through the wheat. Mr. Schiamberg received much media publicity, and he received many congratulatory emails. One MIT employee emailed him, "It took my breath away. All Mondays should be so beautiful." Of course, MIT students added a few touches of their own to the work of art — such as a cow and a scarecrow. However, MIT students liked the field of wheat, and they did not like some of the other works of art on the MIT campus, such as Louise Nevelson's *Transparent Horizons*, which MIT students criticize as being like much other MIT art: In the students' word, the art is "ugly." MIT hackers once installed a desk and a study light in the top of the sculpture, and they once rededicated it with this plaque: "Louise Nevelson / b. 1990 / Big Black Scrap Heap / 1975." And occasionally MIT hackers will install authentic-looking but satiric "works of art" in MIT galleries. For example, in 1985 MIT hacking group James E. Tetazoo installed "NO KNIFE: A STUDY IN MIXED MEDIASEARTH TONES, NUMBER THREE" in MIT's List Visual Arts Center. The "work of art" consisted of a large plate, small plate, fork, two spoons (one a soup spoon), and glass on a tray placed on an upside-down trash receptacle. A statement accompanying the "art" satirized art criticism. The first sentence read, "The artist's mode *d'emploi* relies upon minimalist kinematic methods; space and time are frozen in a staid reality of restrained sexuality."[11]

• Do modern angels wear jeans and use mobile phones? How about statues of modern angels? In the city of Hertogenbosch (aka Den Bosch) in the south of the Netherlands is the Roman Catholic St. John's Cathedral. Dozens of statues are in the medieval cathedral, and some of the statues are recently created. Sculptor Ton Mooy sculpted 25 new angels for the cathedral, and among them he sculpted one modern angel. The artist wanted to create a jet-pack-wearing angel, but that design was rejected, so he created an angel wearing jeans and using a mobile phone. The artist points out, "The phone has just one button. It dials directly to God." (It's also interesting to note that the cathedral also has a large stained-glass window depicting Hell — the window depicts 9-11.)[12]

• British artist Sir Joshua Reynolds looked through some drawings at a second-hand picture dealer's, then asked how much one of the drawings cost. Astonished to hear that the price was 20 guineas, he asked, "Twenty pence, I suppose you mean?" The dealer replied, "No, sir. It is true that this morning I would have taken 20 pence for it, but if you think it is worth looking at, all the world will think it worth buying." Sir Joshua paid the 20 guineas for the drawing.[13]

Audiences

• Sometimes, stand-up comedians face *very* hostile audiences. Once, an audience kept shouting at George Calfa, "Get off! Get off!" He told the audience that the only way he would leave would be for the audience to give him a standing ovation. but after the audience had given him a standing ovation, he told them, "This is the first standing ovation I ever got — I'd better do an encore."[14]

• The recitals of modern dance pioneer Martha Graham were so different from classical ballet that many people had trouble relating to them. A woman attended a Graham recital, then went backstage afterward and asked her, "Martha, how long do you expect to keep up this dreadful dancing?" Ms. Graham replied, "As long as I have an audience."[15]

• CBS executives detested the pilot episode of *Gilligan's Island*; however, when they tested the pilot, they discovered that audiences loved it. This so amazed the CBS executives that they tested the pilot more than once, because they were afraid that something was wrong with the first audience.[16]

• Following the premiere of *Rodeo: The Courting at Burnt Ranch*, choreographed by Agnes de Mille, the cast had 22 curtain calls and was showered with bouquets. Most of the bouquets consisted of flowers, but one was made of ears of corn and red, white, and blue ribbons.[17]

Auditions

• When he was 21, Luigi (Eugene Facciuto) was paralyzed in a car accident. Physicians told him that he would never walk again, but all he could think about was dancing again. An operation on his eyes, which was necessary because the car accident had crushed his head, left him permanently cross-eyed. However, he kept hearing a voice that told him, "Never stop moving, kid. If you stop moving, you're dead. Don't ever stop moving." Through ballet lessons, he was able to rehabilitate himself, and he ended up dancing alongside people such as Gene Kelly. However, he was forced to become a jazz dancer rather than a ballet dancer because his crossed eyes made it impossible for him to perform pirouettes — he couldn't spot. He once auditioned for Lucia Chase and all went well until she asked him to perform some turns in the air. Because of his crossed eyes, he couldn't. He remembers hearing Ms. Chase say, "I thought they said he could dance." As a jazz dancer, he performed with Judy Garland, Leslie Caron, Cyd Charisse, Donald O'Connor, and Vera Ellen. Luigi's most important motto throughout his life has been this: "Never stop moving."[18]

• In April of 1960, a blizzard hit Cincinnati. Young Suzanne Farrell and her mother still made it to an audition for the National Ballet of Canada. However, a chilly journey that lasted over three hours and left no time for Suzanne to warm up took its toll on her and she did not dance well. Still, she says, she danced nowhere near as badly as the National Ballet of Canada told her mother she did. Suzanne says, "I was absolutely crushed. I was ready to give up ballet at fourteen. Then I thought it over, and decided, well, I didn't like that company very much anyway." The very next month New York City Ballet dancer Diana Adams discovered her, and Suzanne received a Ford Foundation Scholarship to study at the School of American Ballet. Of course, Suzanne became a superstar of ballet. By the way, in 1961 a representative of the National Ballet of Canada saw Suzanne taking class and said, "Should you decide to join us ...." Suzanne did not let the representative finish: "Sorry, I have something better to do."[19]

Authors

• When Laura Ingalls Wilder, author of *Little House on the Prairie*, and her husband first arrived at their Rocky Ridge Farm in Missouri, they stayed in a log cabin that had a fireplace but no windows. When they needed more light, they simply knocked out some of the chinking between logs — this let in more light, but it also let in the wind and rain. Later, they built a much nicer house to live in. And while living in Burr Oak, Iowa, she was excited when she found a bullet hole in a door of the hotel where she and her family were living. A husband had gotten drunk, and being angry at his wife, he had tried to shoot her. The wife slammed the door behind her and got away safely.[20]

• As an adult, E.B. White wrote *Charlotte's Web* and *Stuart Little*. When he was a little boy attending his first day of kindergarten, he was annoyed by a little girl who wanted to hold his hand. By the way, as a famous author, Mr. White was often asked to make speeches, but he suffered from stage fright, so he used to decline these invitations by writing, "I am incapable of making a speech." Also by the way, while working at *The New Yorker*, Mr. White declined to come in for regular hours, although he did turn in his work on time. In fact, he once set off for a vacation in Maine — without first informing *The New Yorker*.[21]

• J.R.R. Tolkien was grading a stack of examination papers at Oxford University when he came across an exam that hadn't been completed. In the empty space at the bottom of the exam, he wrote, "In a hole in the ground there lived a hobbit." Later, Mr. Tolkien said, "Names always generate a story in my mind: eventually I thought I'd better find out what hobbits are like." This single sentence at the bottom of an unfinished exam led to Tolkien's books *The Hobbit* and *The Lord of the Rings*.[22]

• A United Kingdom ad for the Yellow Pages shows an old man going to a used bookstore, looking for a copy of *Fly Fishing* by J.R. Hartley. He is unsuccessful, so he goes home and tries the Yellow Pages. Using it, he quickly locates a copy of the book, then while still on the telephone, says, "My name? Oh yes, it's J.R. Hartley." This TV commercial was so successful that a book was created because of it — the book was *Fly Fishing* by — of course — J.R. Hartley.[23]

• Diarmuid Russell and Henry Volkening ran Russell and Volkening Literary Representatives. One of Mr. Volkening's clients advised Bernard Malamud to call up Mr. Volkening and let him be his literary agent, but Mr. Russell became Mr. Malamud's literary agent instead. How did this happen? According to Mr. Russell, "When Bernard called, I answered the phone."[24]

• Comedian Steve Allen — as you would expect — had a sense of humor. The front cover of my copy of his book *More Funny People* shows a photograph of a cleanly shaven Steve Allen. But on the back cover appears a photograph of Mr. Allen's "ghost writer" — the photograph shows a bearded Steve Allen.[25]

• F. Scott Fitzgerald could be disconcerting to talk to. Sometimes during a conversation, he would reach into a pocket, take out a pad of paper, write on it, return it to his pocket, then say, "I just thought of a phrase I didn't want to forget. Now then, what were you saying?"[26]

Bloopers

• Here are a few bloopers: 1) Ed Sullivan once did a quick public service message on his TV program: "And now a word about tuberculosis. Help stamp out TV." 2) On 7 May 1964, President Lyndon Johnson and Ohio Governor James Rhodes came to Athens to help Ohio University celebrate its 160th anniversary. Governor Rhodes got a little mixed up in his choice of words and referred to OU as "this venereal institution." 3) A man whose wife had just had a baby requested a disk jockey to play this song: "I Didn't Know the Gun was Loaded."[27]

• On *Marcus Welby*, the good doctor talked with his son-in-law about his daughter's pregnancy and told him, "Well, at least you're over the hump."[28]

Books

• King Ptolemy III wanted the library at Alexandria to have a copy of every book in the world, even if he had to be unjust to do it. Whenever travelers arrived at Alexandria, their books were confiscated, and if the king wanted to keep a particular book for the library, the traveler was given a poorly and quickly made copy of the book. In addition, he borrowed comedies from the library at Athens and then refused to return them.[29]

• Mark Twain once showed a visitor his library. The visitor commented on the large numbers of books piled everywhere — on the floor, in chairs, everywhere handy. Mr. Twain explained, "It's next to impossible to borrow shelves."[30]

Bridges

• San Francisco's Golden Gate Bridge was completed on May 26, 1937, and the following day was Pedestrian Day — pedestrians were allowed on the bridge. Hundreds of thousands of people showed up, many of whom did silly things. Officials at first thought that one woman was ill, but it turned out that she was trying to be the first person to walk across the bridge with her tongue sticking out. Other firsts on Pedestrian Day were the first person to walk across the bridge on stilts, the first dog to cross the bridge, the first sisters to cross the bridge on roller skates, the first twins to cross the bridge, and the first baby to cross the bridge in a baby carriage. The day after Pedestrian Day was the first day vehicles were allowed to cross the bridge.[31]

• In 1958, MIT students decided to measure the length of the Harvard Bridge using a new kind of measurement: Smoots. A Smoot was the length of first-year student Oliver Smoot, who was a pledge of Lambda Chi fraternity. The fraternity used swimming pool paint to mark each Smoot on the bridge and to write out in full the measurement for every 10 Smoots. The length of the bridge is 364.4 Smoots, plus one ear. Lambda Chi pledges repaint the Smoot markings every two years, and Cambridge, Massachusetts, police use the Smoot markings to indicate exactly where on the bridge an accident took place.[32]

Children

• Kian and Remee are fraternal twins, born in April 2005 a minute apart, although one has black hair and black skin and the other has blonde hair and light skin. At age seven in 2012, they live in Dudley, West Midlands, England. Both twins are biracial, and their parents, Kylee Hodgson and Remi Horder, both have a white mother and a black father. Kylee said, "They are such a perfect example of how it should be. They are not bothered about their skin colour. It's not the big issue everyone else seems to see it as. It isn't important to them at all — it's about what they're like underneath." When Kylee saw them for the first time, she "noticed that both of them had beautiful blue eyes. But while Remee's hair was blonde, Kian's was black and she had darker skin. To me, they were my kids and they were just normal. I thought they would start to look the same as time went on." As time went, however, they looked more different; for example, Kian's eyes grew darker. Kylee said, "People would ask me why I dressed the children the same. I'd just say, 'Because they're twins,' and leave people to work it out. It kind of irritated me at first, but everyone in my area got to know they were twins and accepted it. It was only strangers or outsiders who didn't know." The twins said the same first word: "Juice." However, they are different. According to Kylee, Kian "is a bit bossier, a bit louder. Remee is a bit more laid back. She'll think a bit longer before she does something." Kylee added, "They get on so well. They're really close. They're best friends — they absolutely love each other. They play together all the time, go swimming together, read their books together, help each other out. If one can't do their shoes, the other will help. Sometimes they do the same things at the same time. Once, they even sneezed together. That really made me laugh. As they've got older, they've taught each other everything. They've helped each other to grow. And they don't notice the colour thing, not at all. They've grown up with light-skinned people around them, and they've grown up with black people. But they're just themselves. They don't see what everyone else sees."[33]

• The winter of 1880-1881 was a hard one in De Smet, South Dakota. The snow blizzards covered up the railroad tracks and the train couldn't get through to carry food and fuel to the De Smet residents. Among the families living there was that of Laura Ingalls Wilder, author of *Little House on the Prairie*. In her book *The Long Winter*, she later described her family running out of coal, so she and her father used to twist straw into sticks for fuel. The family also began to run out of food. Fortunately, two young men, Almanzo Wilder and Cap Garland, learned that a certain man had grain stored away. The two young men were able to get grain to distribute to the De Smet families to keep them from starving. Later, young Laura Ingalls married Almanzo Wilder, and much later, when they were elderly, they returned to De Smet for Old Settlers Day and wore badges that said "Hard Winter" to show that they were among the pioneers who had survived the long, hard winter of 1880-1881. By the way, when she was little, Laura and her sisters got measles. Neighboring mothers sent their children to play with the ill little girls so their children would also catch measles and "get it over with."[34]

• When E.B. White was working on his first book for children, *Stuart Little*, he set a deadline for releasing the book in the fall of 1939, but he made sure the publisher knew that this was only a tentative deadline, saying, "Everything depends on whether the finished product turns out pleasing to mine eye. I would rather wait a year than publish a bad children's book, as I have too much respect for children." By the way, in 1961, nine years after E.B. White had published *Charlotte's Web*, a young reader wrote him to ask why he hadn't written another children's book since then. Mr. White was feeling testy that day, and he complained that he would have more time to write children's books if only children would stop writing him letters. However, this doesn't mean that Mr. White disliked children. Sometimes, they sent him awards and certificates, and Mr. White treasured these.[35]

• Child actress Vera Beringer played the lead role in Francis Hodgson Burnett's play version of *Little Lord Fauntleroy* in London. At the conclusion of the opening night performance, Ms. Hodgson threw Vera a bouquet of roses and exclaimed, "Bless the child, and she did not forget a single word!" Later, Vera was able to meet some members of the royal family. She wasn't sure whether to curtsey because she was a girl or bow because she was dressed as a boy. As it turned out, she didn't have to do either because Prince Edward and Princess Alexandra kissed her. By the way, fashions in clothing change over time. In the late 19th century, both infant boys and infant girls wore dresses.[36]

• A boy kept interrupting his father, and to get some peace the father tore out a map of the world from a magazine, tore it into pieces, and told his son to put the world map back together and then come back to him. Since his son did not know geography, his father thought that it would take him a long time to put the world map back together. Quickly, his son returned with the world map put back together correctly. The father asked how his son had put the world back together so quickly. His son said that on the back of the world map was a picture of a child and he had put the pieces of the child back together. Moral: If you want the put the world back together the right way, start with the child.[37]

• A fun activity is to give famous sayings a twist. Begin the famous saying in the usual way, but then give it a different ending. Some elementary-school teachers even give very young students (who don't already know the famous sayings) the beginnings of famous sayings and have them complete the sayings. Some results: 1) The grass is always greener when you remember to water it. 2) If you can't stand the heat, go swimming. 3) It's always darkest before you open your eyes. 4) Better to light a candle than to light an explosive. 5) Laugh, and the world laughs with you. Cry, and someone yells, "Shut up!" 6) Early to bed and early to rise is first in the bathroom.[38]

• Charles Darwin used to keep a couch in his study, and sometimes his children slept there when they were ill. Once, his son Lenny started jumping on the couch. Mr. Darwin said that he didn't want to see him jumping there, so his young son told him, "Then I advise you to go out of the room!" By the way, Mr. Darwin's father was an imposing man. He was six-feet-two inches tall, and he weighed more than 300 pounds. In addition, he sometimes used to give his family lectures that lasted for two hours.[39]

• Modern dance pioneer Martha Graham occasionally taught classes in which little children would imitate the movements of animals. Usually, Ms. Graham could tell which animals the children imitated, but one little girl's movements puzzled her, so she asked, "What animal are you supposed to be?" The little girl replied that she was a bird, but Ms. Graham pointed out that she didn't look as if she were flying. The little girl replied, "I'm a bird eating a worm."[40]

• Katherine Paterson, the author of such children's books as *The Sign of the Chrysanthemum* and *Bridge to Terabithia*, was born in China to parents who were Christian missionaries. Once she returned to the United States, curious children asked her, "If you were born in China, how come you're not Chinese?" Young Katherine replied, "If a cat was born in a garage, does that make it an automobile?"[41]

• Dave McKinley was a retired publisher who once saw his granddaughter deliberately step on an ant, so he lectured her on how wrong it was, because ants were defenseless, and lived in ant farms, and had electricity and running water, and taught us all a lesson about keeping busy, etc. At the end of his lecture, his granddaughter said, "Grandpa, you old son of a b*tch, I love you."[42]

• Astronomer Cecilia Payne-Gaposchkin attended a religious school when she was a child, but she disliked going to chapel everyday. Therefore, she figured out an original way to get out of spending so much time in chapel. She pretended to faint in chapel, and soon the teachers excused her from daily attendance at chapel.[43]

Choreographers

• One must suffer to have the experience to create a credible work of art about suffering. When Gus Solomons, Jr., was a young man, he choreographed his first dance and he put a lot of pain in it. The piece used percussive music, and Mr. Solomons pounded his bare-chested body, exhausting himself in the first three minutes of the dance. When he showed the dance to Murray Louis, Mr. Louis asked, "Gus, what was all that suffering about? What do you know about suffering?"[44]

• Early in his career, while he was still performing in 1959 with Martha Graham's company, Paul Taylor performed a work by George Balanchine titled *Episodes*. Mr. Balanchine told Mr. Taylor that while he was dancing in it he should pretend to be a fly that was trapped in a glass of milk.[45]

Christmas

• Early in life, L. Frank Baum, who later became successful as the writer of *The Wonderful Wizard of Oz*, went bankrupt and lost his newspaper, the Aberdeen *Saturday Pioneer*. He told his friends, "I decided the sheriff wanted the paper more than I did." By the way, Christmas was a special time at the house of Mr. Baum. One year, his house had four Christmas trees placed in the corners of a room — one Christmas tree for each of his children.[46]

• Comedian Jim Carrey's family was funny. On Christmas, sometimes his father, mother, siblings, and Jim himself would go outside, put stockings over their heads, and wave axes at astonished passersby like a bunch of demented axe murderers. Even when he was a kid, Jim knew that he wanted to be a comedian. When he was 10 years old, he sent a resume — a short one — to the producers of *The Carol Burnett Show*. Unfortunately, he never received an answer.[47]

• Actor Sheldon Leonard received interesting compensation for appearing as Nick the bartender in the Christmas classic *It's a Wonderful Life*. He did the part in return for two season tickets to the Dodgers baseball games.[48]

Clothing

• While in Monte Carlo, Ellen Graham's sister needed a formal gown. The prices in Monte Carlo were too high, and she didn't have time to return to her apartment in Paris to pick up one of her own gowns, so Ellen volunteered to lend her something made of shocking pink gossamer. Later, Ellen's friend, comedian Beatrice Lillie, asked her, "Why haven't I seen you in that before?" Ellen replied, "Because it's my nightgown."[49]

• British comedian Victoria Wood says that no TV people ever tried to interfere with her comic material, but they did try to interfere with the clothing she wore — by insisting that she wear dresses, Fed up, she went to the producer and asked, "Excuse me, can I please wear trousers?" He replied, "Yes — don't bother me now." Problem solved.[50]

• A young lieutenant asked General John Pershing to be excused from a parade because his clothing had not yet returned from the laundry. Discovering that the lieutenant needed a white collar and a pair of white gloves, General Pershing lent him the needed clothing, saying, "Here, take these. I washed them myself yesterday."[51]

Chapter 2: From Comedy and Comedians to Food

Comedy and Comedians

• Back when the radio program *Allen's Alley* was popular, its host, comedian Fred Allen, didn't worry too much about ending his show exactly when it was supposed to end. If it ended 45 seconds or even two or three minutes late, that was close enough for him. (These days, when making money from commercials is paramount, the audience would not even hear the end of the show, just a commercial.) *Allen's Alley* was followed by the program *Take It or Leave It*, and midway through the radio season, *Take It or Leave It* suddenly broke into *Allen's Alley*, claiming that it had stolen 15 minutes away from *Take It or Leave It* and therefore *Take It or Leave It* was going to start 15 minutes early and take back all the time that *Allen's Alley* had stolen from it. By the way, Mr. Allen was known for keeping his cool under pressure. On one radio show, he cracked a joke that got only one laugh. Unperturbed, he remarked, "As that one lone laugh goes ricocheting around the studio, we move to a selection by Al Goodman and his orchestra."[52]

• Comedian Myron Cohen loved to tell jokes, including these: 1) A man went to an expensive store, pointed to a one-ounce bottle of perfume on display, and asked how much it cost. The saleswoman replied, "$100." The man whistled, then pointed to another one-ounce bottle of perfume on display and asked how much it cost. The saleswoman replied, "Two whistles." 2) A woman was asked how she got her children to behave so nicely. She replied, "I give my seven-old-year $5, and he's good. And I give my five-year-old $2, and he's good." She was then asked what she gave her three-year-old for him to be good. "Oh," said the woman. "He's like his father — good for nothing."[53]

• Phyllis Diller performed in a fright wig that has hair sticking up everywhere. Early in her career, she used to perform in her own hair. Once, worried about hair loss, she went to a specialist who told her that to stimulate hair growth, she should use a curry comb. She did, and it worked, but it made her hair stand straight up. She went out on stage like that one night, her hair got a laugh, and she started to use fright wigs in her act. In her stand-up comedy act, Ms. Diller carried a long cigarette holder, which she uses to punctuate her jokes. The cigarette in the holder is made of wood — Ms. Diller didn't smoke.[54]

• The British comedy duo French and Saunders — Dawn French and Jennifer Saunders — disliked facing hecklers, and when they thought hecklers would be present they hurried through their act so they could get off stage and avoid them. Once, they went through their 20-minute act in five minutes. On another occasion, they didn't get off the stage on time, so Ms. French used her day job as an educator to put down the heckler by using the persona of a strict teacher: "Excuse me, you prickhead there — now come on! If you don't think it's funny, then leave, but I'm not going to have this talking!"[55]

• Early in his career, comedian Jay Leno met Rahsaan Roland Kirk, a blind African-American jazz musician. They worked together, with Mr. Kirk performing his black nationalist rap in front of a black nationalist audience that was thinking "Get Whitey" throughout his performance. Mr. Kirk then introduced the very Caucasian Mr. Leno as a "brother." This had Mr. Leno worried, but he broke the ice by telling the audience, "Hey, maybe you haven't noticed — Rahsaan's blind." The audience laughed, and Mr. Leno followed with a very funny set.[56]

• American ballerina Nora Kaye used to dance in a satire called *Gala Performance*, in which she would make fun of flashy Russian ballerinas. One day, just before she was to dance this part, a real Russian ballerina danced in a flashy *pas de deux* (a ballet dance for two people). Ms. Kaye watched from the sidelines, then told the director, "Well, she's already done the part, and short of taking my teeth out and tossing them over the footlights, I can't think of any way to make this look like a comedy."[57]

• Monty Python member Graham Chapman was an original from early in his life. As a child, he once placed a chair in the kitchen sink, then sat on it in order to gain a different perspective. As an adult, Mr. Chapman was known for being late for everything. When he and John Cleese wrote sketches together, they would meet at one or the other's house, and Mr. Chapman always managed to arrive half an hour late — even when they were meeting at his own house.[58]

• Stand-up comedian Jay Leno once worked at Cleveland's Front Row Theater. He tried to get a room at a nearby motel, but the manager's wife explained that all the rooms were booked. Just then, a loud commotion arose, caused by the motel manager yelling at and kicking out musician Stephen Stills. Mr. Stills said, "Hey, Jay." Mr. Leno said, "Hey, Stephen." The manager's wife said, "I think something just opened up."[59]

• Lord Buckley was a 1950s comedian who said pretty much whatever he wanted, whether the audience wanted to hear it or not. Once, a big man started to heckle him, so Lord Buckley asked him to step outside. They did, and a few minutes later, the two men returned. The heckler was unharmed, but Lord Buckley had been stomped. Lord Buckley then continued his act as if nothing had happened.[60]

• Normally, Jack Benny was not funny without his writers, but at least once he got off a funny ad lib. It happened when he was a guest on Fred Allen's radio show, and Mr. Allen — who was funny with or without writers — was zinging Mr. Benny with ad-lib comic insults. Finally, Mr. Benny blurted out, "You wouldn't dare say that if my writers were here."[61]

• Before becoming a comedian, Roseanne used to work as a waitress and insult her customers. After someone ordered, she would say such things as "Those drinks are gonna be six bucks, and it'll cost you three more to have me take 'em off the tray and put 'em on the table." She was so good that customers came in just so she could insult them.[62]

• After comedian Margaret Cho became famous, one of the people who had emotionally tortured her when they were children came to one of her shows, walked up to her backstage afterwards, and asked her, "Do you remember me?" She replied, "No, I don't. I have absolutely no idea who you are," and then she walked away.[63]

• It's hard to put on Jonathan Winters. Pat Harrington, Jr., used to pretend to be an Italian golf pro with the name Guido Panzini. While in character, he would go up to unsuspecting people and give them golf tips. Once, he went up to Mr. Winters, who looked him over, said "Irish," then walked away.[64]

• Comedian Larry Miller once opened for Frank Sinatra in Las Vegas. Before showtime, Mr. Sinatra walked into his dressing room just as Mr. Miller was pulling up his pants. As Mr. Miller reached to shake hands, his pants fell to the floor and he let them remain there until Mr. Sinatra left. Mr. Miller says, "He was very cool — he didn't say a word about it."[65]

• Stand-up comedian Judy Tenuta once worked in a dive so bad that a rat ran across the stage when she was introduced. The owner of the dive killed it — by shooting it with a .357 Magnum.[66]

Critics

• Music critic Henry T. Finck enjoyed collecting anecdotes and stories. For example: 1) Lilli Lehmann used an interesting method to teach Geraldine Farrar how to act without the use of extravagant hand gestures. She would tie Ms. Farrar's hands behind her back, and then say to her, "Now express your feelings." 2) Some artists dislike encores. Conductor Arturo Toscanini was one. On occasion, so was Enrico Caruso. Once, members of an audience kept clapping their hands, yelling, and stamping their feet because they wanted an encore of "*Una fertiva lagrima*." Mr. Caruso did not wish to oblige. He kept saying, "Hush," to the audience, which ignored him. Finally, he carried a chair onto the stage and sat in it with his back to the audience until he was able to continue without singing an encore. 3) The Australian explorer Carl Lumholtz once told Mr. Finck about an encounter with a cannibal who asked him to walk in back because when Mr. Lumholtz walked in front, the cannibal was tempted to put a spear in his back and make a meal of him. Mr. Finck and Mr. Lumholtz once ate supper together; the main dish was terrapin liver, a delicacy, but Mr. Lumholtz confessed that it was good, but he liked python liver better.[67]

• The inaugural performance of the Metropolitan Opera in Lincoln Center was an opera by an American composer: Samuel Barber's *Antony and Cleopatra*. Unfortunately, the performance was critically panned. Even before the performance, Sir Rudolf Bing knew that the production was likely to be a failure. When he met soprano Leontyne Price's mother just before the performance, she said, "I had envisioned you as a much larger man." Sir Rudolf replied, "Until a week ago, I was."[68]

• The people who make money from dance and the people who criticize dance sometimes have somewhat different perceptions of the role of dance criticism. Dance impresario Sol Hurok once told dance critic Clive Barnes, "You know, Clive, the critic's job is to sell tickets." He replied, "Sol, you are absolutely right, but we get to choose the tickets we feel are worth selling."[69]

• A critic objected to George Balanchine's choreography of *Apollo* and asked him, "Young man, where did you ever see Apollo walking on his knees?" Refusing to be intimidated, Mr. Balanchine replied, "I would ask you: Where did you ever see Apollo?"[70]

Dance and Dancers

• American dance pioneer Ted Shawn once choreographed the bawdy ancient Greek comedy *Lysistrata*, in which the Spartan and Athenian women decide to stop the Peloponnesian War by declining to have sex with their husbands until the war ends. His choreography for the dance was "hot," and this upset some members of the audience, including one person who said, "A man and woman lying on the floor together have only one thing on their minds!" Mr. Shawn replied, "The man and woman do have just one thing on their minds, and the problem of the ballet was to show it beautifully, which I think I've done." Unfortunately, the threat of being hurt at the box office led Mr. Shawn to tone down the sexuality of the dance, something he neglected to tell dancer Myrna Pace. While dancing the role, Ms. Pace of course noticed the changes in the way Mr. Shawn was dancing and joked, "Don't you love me anymore?"[71]

• Ballerina Tanaquil Le Clercq paid no attention to the superstition that it is bad luck to whistle in a dressing room, but she once shared a dressing room with a ballerina who did. Because the only way to get rid of the bad luck is to go outside the dressing room and twirl three times, Ms. Le Clercq says that "for one whole season I spent more time twirling off stage than on."[72]

• Dancer/comedian Norma Miller spent a busy life in show business, and she never married. Late in her life, men would occasionally ask her why she had never married, and she would tell them, "Because none of you bastards ever asked me!"[73]

Death

• In 1728, Benjamin Franklin wrote this epitaph: "The Body of / B. Franklin Printer, / (Like the Cover of an old Book / Its Contents tore out / And stript of its Lettering & Gilding,) / Lies here, Food for Worms. / But the Work shall not be lost; / For it will, (as he believ'd) appear once more, / In a new and more elegant Edition / Revised and corrected, / By the Author." Actually, this epitaph was created as a writing exercise. Mr. Franklin's grave in Philadelphia has no epitaph; it bears only his name. By the way, the children of some of Mr. Franklin's British friends owned a squirrel named Skugg. When Skugg died, Mr. Franklin composed this epitaph for him: "Here lies Skugg, as Snug as a Bug in a Rug." Also by the way, Mr. Franklin was a master of the put-on. He once wrote this in a letter that was published in the London *Public*

Advertiser: "Whales, when they have a Mind to eat Cod, pursue them wherever they fly; and the grand leap of the Whale in that Chace up the Fall of Niagara is esteemed by all who have seen it, as one of the finest Spectacles in Nature!"[74]

• Even in death, people can be witty. The obituary for Michael 'Flathead' Blanchard (1944-2012) in the *Denver Post* on 12 April 2012 stated, "A Celebration of the life of Michael 'Flathead' Blanchard will be held on April 14th, 3 pm 8160 Rosemary St, Commerce City [Colorado]. Weary of reading obituaries noting someone's courageous battle with death, Mike wanted it known that he died as a result of being stubborn, refusing to follow doctors' orders and raising hell for more than six decades. He enjoyed booze, guns, cars and younger women until the day he died. [...] Baba Yaga can kiss his butt. So many of his childhood friends that weren't killed in Vietnam went on to become criminals, prostitutes and/or Democrats. He asks that you stop by and re-tell the stories he can no longer tell. As the Celebration will contain Adult material we respectfully ask that no children under 18 attend."[75]

• The book jacket of *Graham Crackers*, a compilation of humorous bits written by Monty Python's Graham Chapman, shows photographs of how Mr. Chapman looked at age 12 and how he looks today. The "today" photograph shows a funerary urn — Mr. Chapman died on 4 October 1989, the day before Monty Python celebrated its 20th anniversary. According to fellow Python member Terry Jones, Mr. Chapman's death was "the worst case of party-pooping I've ever seen." Even after Mr. Chapman died, the other members of the comedy group did not forget him. At a Python meeting after his death, he was given a vote — his spirit was asked to rap once for yes, twice for no. (Mr. Graham abstained.)[76]

• After Thomas Jefferson took over for Benjamin Franklin in France, he was asked, "It is you, sir, who replace Doctor Franklin?" Mr. Jefferson always answered, "No one can replace him, sir; I am only his successor." By the way, Mr. Jefferson wrote his own epitaph: "Author of the Declaration of Independence, of the Statute of Virginia for religious freedom and Father of the University of Virginia." He also charged his heirs to obey his wishes: "Not a word more."[77]

Education

• While attending Homestead High School in Cupertino, California, Stephen Wozniak found the electronics classes to be very easy, so his teacher, John McCollum, arranged for him to spend Wednesday afternoons in the computer room of GTE/Sylvania Electronics, where young Steve was able to learn something about electronics. Steve built a computer in a friend's garage. While working on the computer, he and his friend drank quarts of cream soda so they decided to call the computer the Cream Soda Computer. When the computer was built, Steve's mother called a newspaper to come out, take a photograph, and write a story. Unfortunately, when Steve turned on the computer, sparks and smoke filled the air. The story was never published, but Steve didn't mind since he knew the fault was not his. Instead, the disaster occurred because of a faulty computer chip. Later, Mr. Wozniak co-founded the Apple Computer Company.[78]

• As a student in elementary and high school, Bill Cosby was lacking — although he did go on to earn a doctorate in education at the University of Massachusetts in 1976. Often, before he became serious about getting an education, he would read a comic book in class instead of his textbooks. Sometimes, he would get caught, and the teacher would take the comic book away, saying, "You'll get this back at the end of the school year." Bill would then ask the teacher, "Why? Does it take that long to read it?" By the way, early in his career, comedian Mr. Cosby played a club that was so small that it didn't have a stage. Instead, management placed a chair on top of a table and Mr. Cosby did his act from there.[79]

• For the first time, a young novice went out of the monastery, but in the company of an old Buddhist monk. The novice saw a young woman selling vegetables, and he asked the old monk, "What is that?" The old monk replied, "A tiger." Later, the novice saw a real tiger, and he asked, "What is that?" The old monk replied, "A young woman." When the novice and the old monk had returned to the monastery, the head of the monastery, knowing that the novice had seen a woman and a tiger on his trip outside, decided to test the novice. He asked the novice, "What did you like best of all the things you saw outside the monastery?" The novice replied, "The tiger."[80]

• When comedian Kate Clinton was a teacher of "at-risk" children, a nun came in to observe her class. Ms. Clinton knew the nun was going to observe her, so she alerted all her students to come to class on time — especially one student who was notorious for his tardiness. The student stayed up late the night before to watch a baseball game, forgot about the nun, came to class tardy as usual, and said, "The f — ing Yankees suck." Then he noticed the nun and looked at Ms. Clinton, who told him, "Steve, you need to apologize to the class for what you said." Steve said, "I'm sorry I said 'suck.' Twice."[81]

• Comedian Jay Leno declines to act as if he is better than other people. Once, while boarding a plane, he pushed himself in front of an old lady in a wheelchair, who waved him on and said, "Oh, go ahead, dearie." This made him feel terrible. He said, "I felt like the guy on the *Titanic* who puts on a dress so he can get in the life raft first." After that, he acted like a normal person instead of like a big shot. By the way, in 1968, comedian Jay Leno graduated from Andover (Massachusetts) High School. In his yearbook, he wrote that he wanted his future career to be "retired millionaire."[82]

• Sometimes, dancers can do more than they think they are capable of. When choreographing to the music of *Ballade for Piano and Orchestra*, George Balanchine named a sequence of steps for Merrill Ashley to dance. She and all the dancers watching the session laughed because they thought that that particular sequence of steps was much too difficult for anyone to do. However, dancers want to please Mr.

Balanchine, so Ms. Ashley attempted the steps — and nailed them on her first attempt! Then she repeated the successful execution of the steps![83]

• Choreographer George Balanchine educated his dancers. Frequently, he told them, "Don't relax! The time to relax is in the grave." In addition, he would work hard to get a dancer to perform a step correctly. Frequently, the dancer would say about a difficult step, "I'll try." Mr. Balanchine would reply, "Don't try — just do!" When the dancer had succeeded, he would say, "That's right!" Then he would add, "But now, dear, make it beautiful."[84]

• Some elementary schoolteachers have uncontrollable kids. A teacher in Marblehead, Massachusetts, once told a mother that her son was "the worst brat in 10 states." The mother responded that the schoolteacher was "repressing her boy's natural vivaciousness." However, the schoolteacher did not believe that; instead, she responded that the next time the boy bit her she would send "him home in a cage."[85]

• When George Balanchine choreographed, he sometimes did more than create a beautiful dance. Often, he choreographed as a way to teach other people. For example, he knew that Jerome Robbins was a wonderful choreographer, but that his dance training in the classical style was weak, so he choreographed *Caracole* and put Mr. Robbins in it as a way to train him in the classical style of dancing.[86]

• Lincoln Kirstein once took dance lessons from Michel Fokine in Paris, but he demonstrated little dancing ability. Later, Mr. Kirstein and George Balanchine created the School of American Ballet (and the company that became the New York City Ballet), causing Mr. Fokine to ask, "How can Kirstein be the director of a ballet company? He took some ballet lessons from me, and he can't get his feet off the floor!"[87]

• Giacomo Puccini began to learn how to play the piano in an interesting way. His father put coins on certain keys of the piano, and in grabbing the coins, the young Giacomo pounded out a tune. By the way, the favorite opera of King George V of England was Puccini's *La Boheme*. When asked why it was his favorite, he replied, "Because it's much the shortest."[88]

• When the Dance Theatre of Harlem was first started, classes took place in a garage on 140th Street and St. Nicholas Avenue. During the summer, the garage doors were opened up. Occasionally, passersby would become intrigued by the dance classes and watch — and sometimes sign up to become students themselves.[89]

• Trinity College at the University of Cambridge is known for its arrogance. When one of its Fellows won a Nobel Prize, the Master began his speech by saying, "Anywhere else, I could say that this is a very special occasion."[90]

• One of rocker Rod Stewart's major influences was gospel and pop singer Sam Cooke. In fact, Mr. Stewart once spent two years listening to Mr. Cooke and only Mr. Cooke.[91]

Fans

• Comedian Bob Hope was a big fan of Charlie Chaplin and when he was young, he even won a contest doing a Chaplin imitation. In New York, a friend told him that Mr. Chaplin's car was parked outside a restaurant, so Mr. Hope waited around for 90 minutes just to catch a glimpse of Mr. Chaplin.[92]

• When Napoleon was traveling to his coronation, people turned out to see him and to cheer for him. Napoleon looked at the crowd, then said that exactly the same people would turn out to see him if he were on his way to the guillotine.[93]

Food

• As a stand-up comedian, Jay Leno has traveled all over the United States, and he sometimes comes across odd things. While in West Virginia, he stopped at a restaurant whose menu listed a "Wop Salad." Mr. Leno asked what a Wop Salad was, and the waiter said it was a regular salad served with Italian dressing. And at an "Italian" restaurant in Iowa, Jay Leno ordered spaghetti and meatballs, and the waiter asked him, "You want fries with that?"[94]

• George Burns was Jewish, and his wife, Gracie Allen, was Catholic. They raised their adopted children, Ronald and Sandy, Catholic. Every Friday, the Burns family ate fish, as Catholics at that time did. Sandy did not like fish, so she ate elsewhere on Fridays and told people that she was a Catholic only six days a week.[95]

• Theatrical producer Jed Harris once made an appointment to meet playwright Charles MacArthur at a restaurant for lunch, but showed up 10 hours late, just as the restaurant was closing. He asked Mr. MacArthur if he had been waiting long. Mr. MacArthur replied, "No, I just got here a couple of hours ago myself."[96]

• How much would the best meal in the world cost? How about $4,000? That's how much Parisian chef Denis Lahana charged Craig Claiborne and a friend for a meal consisting of 31 dishes, 9 wines, cognac, and Calvados. (The bill was paid by American Express, which used the meal as a publicity stunt.)[97]

• Gioacchino Rossini was a big eater. Unfortunately, he once dined at the home of a host who served small portions. After the dinner of small portions had been served, his host said, "I do hope you will soon do us the honor of dining here again." Mr. Rossini replied, "Certainly. Let's start now."[98]

• Ballerina Marie Taglioni was so beloved that a group of ballet lovers in Russia boiled her toe shoes, then ate them. In her youth, Ms. Taglioni had been round-shouldered, and one of her dance teachers said that she didn't know "what to do with that little hunchback."[99]

• Shortly after coming to the United States for the first time, choreographer George Balanchine fell ill. He recovered, apparently helped by a high-calorie, high-cholesterol diet. All the eggs, cream, and butter he ate resulted in a weight gain of 30 pounds in 30 days.[100]

Chapter 3: From Friends to Money

Friends

• Jack Benny was George Burns' best friend and best audience: Mr. Burns could always make Mr. Benny laugh. Once, Mr. Benny complained about not sleeping well. Mr. Burns asked, "How did you sleep the night before?" Mr. Benny replied, "The night before I slept great." Mr. Burns then advised, "Try sleeping every other night." And once, Mr. Burns said absolutely nothing, and Mr. Benny started laughing. Mr. Burns asked why Mr. Benny was laughing; after all, he (Mr. Burns) had not said a word. Mr. Benny replied, "I know. But you didn't say it on purpose."[101]

• Bertrand Russell and Ludwig Wittgenstein were not only professor and student, but also friends. Still, Mr. Wittgenstein could be an exasperating student. For example, Mr. Russell once said of him, "He thinks nothing empirical is knowable." Mr. Russell had good reason for making this statement. Mr. Wittgenstein had refused to acknowledge the truth of the statement "There is no rhinoceros in this lecture room" — even after Mr. Russell had looked all through the lecture room for a rhinoceros, even checking under tables and chairs.[102]

Games

• Both Jim Backus and Alan Hale, who played Thurston Howell III and the Skipper on *Gilligan's Island*, were avid golfers. Once, they made a bet about who could drive a golf ball further, so they started hitting golf balls on the CBS back lot. They were too lazy to walk out to see who had driven the ball further, so they argued about it, with Mr. Backus claiming, "My ball went at least 10 yards further than yours." Just then, a security guard came up to them and announced that one of the golf balls had gone through the window of a car in the parking lot. Mr. Backus immediately pointed to Mr. Hale and said, "He outdrove me by a mile!"[103]

• An Athenian once saw Aesop, teller of fables, entertaining some children and playing games with them. Aesop was laughing and enjoying himself. The Athenian, however, did not approve and told Aesop that grown-ups should not waste their time in such a way. Aesop then pointed to the Athenian's bow and asked if sometimes he unstrung it. "Yes," the Athenian replied, "if a bow is never unstrung, it will lose its elasticity and become useless." Aesop said, "The same is true of people."[104]

• Herbert Ransom was an actor who was a terrible poker player whose face always showed whether he had a good hand or a bad hand. Because Mr. Ransom was so bad, fellow poker player Franklin Pierce Adams once proposed a new rule: "Anyone who looks at Ransom's face is cheating."[105]

Gays and Lesbians

• Lesbian comedian Judy Carter knows a lot about homosexuality: 1) She learned that not all stereotypes are true when she met and got to know a big butch lesbian who had both a tough attitude and a pink bedroom, complete with doll collection and lace bedspread. 2) She knows that people discover that they are gay at different ages. For example, she knows Mary Newman, who was a grandmother when she became attracted to another woman. At age 64, she left her husband and moved in with the woman she loved. 3) A homophobe once said to Ms. Carter, "The Bible says, 'If a man lies with a man as one lies with a woman ... he must be put to death' (Leviticus 20:13)." She replied, "It also says in the Bible that 'he who touches a pig must be put to death,' and also that 'he who wears clothing woven of two kinds of materials shall be put to death.' So if you want to be literal, no more NFL (touching pigskin = death) and no more poly-cotton blends. And it wasn't us gays who invented polyester!"[106]

• Some homosexuals have been devoted to dance, including Sergey Diaghilev, who organized the Ballets Russes. One day, while watching a rehearsal of George Balanchine's *Apollo*, he turned to Mr. Balanchine and said, "How beautiful." Thinking Mr. Diaghilev was talking about the music, Mr. Balanchine agreed, but Mr. Diaghilev said, "No, no. I mean [Serge] Lifar's *ss; it is like a rose."[107]

• A young gay man was so impressed by *Bewitched*'s Endora (played by the brilliant actress Agnes Moorehead) that when he was surrounded by bullies in a schoolyard he threw a curse on them: "Bat's wings, cow's eyes, the moon in eclipse! Make them as effeminate as Quentin Crisp!"[108]

• When comedian Kate Clinton was growing up, her sister sometimes called her "a big fat queer." When Ms. Clinton grew up, she discovered that she was a lesbian. Nowadays, hoping that history will repeat itself, her sister calls her "a big fat millionaire."[109]

Good Deeds

• In early 2012 an oarsman on the crew team of Columbia University came out as a gay man to his father, who gave him an ultimatum: change his sexual orientation with the help of a Catholic "reparative therapy" program (and keep receiving college tuition from his father) or else his father would have nothing further to do with him (including giving him college tuition). The oarsman told his coach, an openly gay man, about this situation, and the coach contacted the financial aid office to arrange for an emergency appointment for the oarsman. Columbia gave the oarsman a full work-study financial aid package. The oarsman is no longer an oarsman due to lack of time — work-study does take time — but it is much better than not being able to go to college.[110]

• As a child growing up in Texas, African-American choreographer Alvin Ailey discovered a huge snake living under his family's house. Everyday, he fed the snake some of his own food. Unfortunately, this happened during hard times for his family when both money and food were difficult to acquire. His mother was not pleased to learn what he was doing with the food that she had worked so hard to provide for him. A good deed that did work out occurred when Alvin was taking lessons in tuba in the fourth grade. His school principal learned that Alvin's family could not afford to pay for the tuba, so the principal paid for it and gave it to Alvin. (Sometimes, the mnemonic spelling aid "The principal is a pal" is accurate.)[111]

• When Randy Cox of Gladewater, Texas, was diagnosed with cancer in early 2012, his son, Drew Cox, age six, wanted to help. The family had medical insurance, but out-of-pocket expenses would still amount to thousands of dollars, so on 14 April 2012 Drew set up a lemonade stand outside their home to raise money. Drew said about his father, "He is so important to me. We like to play with each other. Lots of times we like to play games." He charged 25 cents for lemonade, but many customers paid much more than that. One customer even wrote a check for $5,000! People came from far away to buy lemonade. By the end of the day, Drew had raised over $10,000 to help pay his father's medical bills.[112]

Illnesses and Injuries

• Humor writer Robert Benchley once became ill and summoned a physician, who prescribed a new medication for him, although Mr. Benchley was worried about possible side effects. The next day the physician made a house call (this was a long time ago) and asked Mr. Benchley, who was lying in bed, how he was doing. "Fine," said Mr. Benchley, "but I don't quite know what to make of this — is this all right?" Then Mr. Benchley pulled down his blanket, revealing his thighs, to which he had glued the feathers from one of his pillows.[113]

• Once, when he knew she would be dressed, actor Bruce Laffey knocked on comedian Beatrice Lillie's door and started to open the door. He was surprised when she slammed the door shut in his face. When she opened the door a few moments later, she was throwing perfume in the air. Mr. Laffey asked what was wrong, and Ms. Lillie told him, "I just farted." By the way, Ms. Lillie had an operation for hemorrhoids, then met her physician at a party; however, he didn't recognize her. Apologizing, he said, "I don't remember faces."[114]

• W.W. Jacobs, the author of *Many Cargoes*, met G.K. Chesterton at a dinner where Mr. Chesterton confessed to him that he had rheumatism and did not know how he was going to be able to give his speech. Mr. Chesterton solved his problem by leaning heavily on Mr. Jacobs' shoulder while giving the speech. Later, Mr. Jacobs said that the speech was good, but it seemed to him to be the longest speech he had ever sat through.[115]

Insults

• Sir Rudolf Bing, the general manager of the Metropolitan Opera, disliked union negotiations, especially when the union negotiators were loud in making their demands. He once said to one such union negotiator, "I'm awfully sorry. I didn't get that. Would you mind screaming it again?" On another occasion, a negotiator asked Sir Rudolf, "Are you trying to show your contempt for the way I conduct a bargaining session?" He replied, "On the contrary, I am trying very hard to conceal it."[116]

• William Randolph Hearst and Marion Davies lived together although they were unmarried; however, they refused to let visitors to their San Simeon mansion do as they did. Dorothy Parker visited San Simeon, did as Mr. Hearst and Ms. Davies did, and was disinvited to the mansion. On her way out, she wrote in the guestbook: "Upon my honor / I saw a Madonna / Standing in a niche / Above the door / Of the famous wh*re / Of a prominent son of a b*tch."[117]

• When Sir Larry Lamb was editor of the *Daily Express*, he suffered a serious heart attack. Fortunately, the distinguished surgeon Gareth Rees saved his life by operating on him for nine hours. Afterward, a member of Sir Larry's staff was quoted (anonymously) as saying that the operation had lasted so long because Dr. Rees had needed eight hours simply to locate Sir Larry's heart.[118]

Language

• While entertaining in India, English entertainer Joyce Grenfell collected personals in Indian newspapers, including this one:

"Engagement. Mr F. d'Cunha (Lallee) of Byculla is to get buckled up to Miss Valierien shortly." Also while in India, Ms. Joyce Grenfell saw many beggars. One beggar wore a sign saying "Help this poor lame." Another beggar wore a sign saying "Pleseh elp this Poor dumb." And while entertaining in the Middle East, Ms. Grenfell heard one of her hosts described as a M.T.F. When she asked what that meant, she learned that it stood for "Must Touch Flesh."[119]

• While in San Francisco, Mark Twain undertook to learn French. One day, a Frenchman who knew no English started asking questions of a group Mr. Twain was in. Because Mr. Twain was the only person in the group who had studied French, he listened to the Frenchman. However, before Mr. Twain had said a half-dozen words of French in reply, the Frenchman fainted, possibly from hunger. Mr. Twain got food for the Frenchman, but said later, "I'll learn French if it kills every Frenchman in the country."[120]

• Alexander Woollcott and Harpo Marx were in a Paris hotel where Harpo upset the management with his shenanigans. Mr. Woollcott tried explaining Harpo to the management, but gave it up, turned to Harpo, and said, "How can I explain you? There's no French word for 'boob.'"[121]

• Ring Lardner once read through a newspaper column about the 10 most beautiful words in the English language — words such as "moonlight," "melody," and "tranquil." Setting the newspaper down, he mused, "What's wrong with 'gangrene'?"[122]

• French grammarian Dominique Bonhours cared about language even on his deathbed. As he lay dying, he said, "I am about to — or I am going to — die; either expression is used."[123]

Letters

• In 1975, publishing company Alfred A. Knopf rejected *A River Runs Through It and Other Stories* by Norman Maclean, although it had previously said that it would publish the book. University of Chicago Press published the book, which met with considerable critical praise and popular success. Much later, an Alfred A Knopf editor wrote Mr. Maclean to express interest in seeing the manuscript of his next book. However, Mr. Maclean was still sore — very sore — over being rejected by Alfred A Knopf in the past, and he still dreamed of telling off the publishing company, so for his reply letter he wrote a masterpiece of invective that ended with "if the situation ever arose when Alfred A. Knopf was the only publishing house remaining in the world and I was the sole remaining author, that would mark the end of the world of books." Mr. Maclean called his letter "one of the best things I ever wrote [...] I really told those bastards off. What a pleasure! What a pleasure! Right into my hands! Probably the only dream I ever had in life that came completely true."[124]

• When poet Nikki Giovanni was a very young girl, she attended an all-black Episcopal school called St. Simon's in Cincinnati. After the mother of a teacher died, the school principal asked Nikki's class to write letters of condolence to the teacher. Young Nikki wrote, "I'm sorry your mother died. But it's just one of those things." This letter was never mailed — Nikki's teacher told her, "We can't say *that*." By the way, when Ms. Giovanni was young, much segregation existed in the United States. She eagerly awaited the coming of the Disney movie *Snow White and the Seven Dwarves* to Knoxville, Tennessee, but she was disappointed when it arrived first at the whites-only movie theater. She and other children with her skin color had to wait for it to come to the blacks-only theater before they could see it.[125]

• A person who posts online as Revstephmc tells about not living close to her only niece, Brooke, but sending her a letter each week, beginning when Brooke was two. The letters are known as "Thursday letters" because that is the day she writes them. When Brooke was two years old, she talked with Revstephmc's mother: "Auntie Steph writes me a letter every week." Revstephmc's mother asked, "That's a lot of letters. What does she write about?" Brooke replied, "She tells me that she loves me! Sometimes she says it long and sometimes she says it short!" Revstephmc says, "She was absolutely right!"[126]

• Moss Hart apparently was curious about other people's mail and was known to read his friends' letters if they were lying around or were in unsealed envelopes. To cure his friend of this bad habit, Alexander Woollcott once put this letter in an unsealed envelope and left it where he knew Mr. Hart would find it: "I'll ask you up here just as soon as I can get rid of this nauseating Moss Hart, who hangs on like a leech, although he knows how I detest him."[127]

• Corey Ford once wrote a letter to Frank Sullivan in which he described being in a plane over the Atlantic when the engine caught on fire. Mr. Sullivan was unsympathetic: "What better place for an engine to catch fire? You have the whole d*mn Atlantic to put it out with!"[128]

Media

• When geneticist Barbara McClintock won the 1983 Nobel Prize in Physiology or Medicine, she was surrounded by reporters who wanted to interview her. At a press conference, a reporter asked her, "What do you think of big to-dos like this, with all the attention that's being heaped upon you?" The 81-year-old geneticist replied, "You put up with it."[129]

• Richard Watson, author of *The Philosopher's Diet*, suggests that people look at the models in a fashion magazine, then look at the models in *Playboy* or *Playgirl*. The exercise should show that people enjoy looking at skinny bodies with some clothes on them, while they enjoy looking at naked bodies with some meat on them.[130]

Mishaps

• Ana Samways writes a column titled "Sideswipe" in the *New Zealand Herald*; her column is a collection of funny photographs and anecdotes that her readers send her. For example, a parent wrote about her daughter, who is a Good Samaritan, "One morning in Bondi [New South Wales, Australia], she spotted from behind what appeared to be a toddler about to cross a busy road and no sign of mum! Quick as a flash, with her long legs and high heels flying, she darted through the traffic and whisked the unattended toddler off his feet ... But the 'toddler' was a very disgruntled dwarf who swore at her." In the same column, Ms. Samways put an anecdote sent in by Erik Wetting, who has a female friend who works as a Quarantine Officer at Auckland International Airport in New Zealand. A young female passenger who was returning to New Zealand had been hiking while abroad, and hiking boots need to be inspected for such things as soil and seeds because the seeds of a plant non-native to New Zealand could disrupt the ecology. Mr. Wetting's friend told the young female passenger, "Show me your boots." He writes that the passenger "stared blankly at my friend for a moment and then with a shrug started to remove her T-shirt and bra." The Quarantine Officer quickly let the passenger know, "I said, 'BOOTS.'"[131]

• After stand-up comedian Judy Carter accepted an invitation to perform in front of a group of handicapped children, she worked hard on her act, which consisted of comic magic tricks involving such things as floating food, but when she arrived at the performance site, she discovered that the children's handicap was blindness. She ended up improvising her act, telling the children that she was completely naked and how cold it was on stage. Ms. Carter also once worked on a revolving stage. Big mistake. Each time she reached a punch line, she was facing a new part of the audience — who did not know what she was talking about.[132]

• Author G.K. Chesterton once visited Oxford, where he made an acquaintance of an undergraduate, Philip Guedalla, even going to visit him in his rooms. During the visit, Mr. Chesterton sat in Mr. Guedalla's only armchair — being very much overweight, he broke it. In addition, Mr. Chesterton drank all of Mr. Guedalla's whiskey. Mr. Guedalla asked him to autograph a copy of *Orthodoxy*, and Mr. Chesterton wrote, "BOSH BY G.K. CHESTERTON." By the way,

Mr. Chesterton once belonged to a debating society with the name of I.D.F. The initials stand for "I Don't Know."[133]

• Very early in his career, during an open-mike night, stand-up comedian Greg Dean made the mistake of inviting a heckler on stage to see if he could get laughs. The heckler told a very funny joke, and even though the club manager succeeded in getting the heckler off stage, the manager then yelled at Mr. Dean, "There are tons of people who have signed up to get on this stage. You can't put anyone you want up here. Don't ever do that again. Now finish your show." For the next six months, Mr. Dean was too mortified to do stand-up.[134]

• Steeply raked (that is, steeply sloped) stages can cause disasters. At a 1962 production of Johann Strauss' *Die Fledermaus* at the Deutsche Oper am Rhein in Cologne, Germany, a piano was wheeled on stage so it could be played at the party given by the character Prince Orlovsky. Somehow, the piano slipped, and it headed down the stage directly into the orchestra pit. Fortunately, the musicians got out of the way in time to avoid injury, but two tubas were flattened and the piano was demolished.[135]

• Entertainer Phil Baker was bald and wore a hairpiece. Once, while they were working together on the movie *Goldwyn Follies*, the very distinguished Adolphe Menjou saw Mr. Baker and told him, "My God, where did you get that piece? Wardrobe will take advantage of a newcomer every time. You go right back there and tell them to give you a decent hairpiece." Unfortunately, Mr. Baker's hairpiece did not come from wardrobe — it was his own personal property.[136]

• Operatic tenor Leo Slezak was a big man — six-foot-four and 300 pounds. Once, while singing the role of Adolar in Weber's *Euryanthe*, he accidentally stepped on a female singer's toes. She had to stay in bed for a month and lost all the toenails on one foot. Whenever he saw the singer, Ms. Ludmilla, afterward, she always took one step backward, then said, "Take my soul, my life, my all — but for God's sake take care not to tread on my toes, dear Adolar!"[137]

• Unfortunately, at some operas, the music and the singers don't finish at the same time. Orchestra leader Gottfried Schmidt once told of finishing five full seconds before the singers in the second act of a 1981 performance of *Carmen*. In fact, Mr. Schmidt boasted, "Next time we shall beat them by 10 seconds."[138]

• Ballerinas have amazing flexibility. Tanaquil Le Clerq once showed up for practice with a bandage on her nose. Why? She had practiced a forward kick (a *grand battement*) — and she had karate-kicked herself right in the nose![139]

Money

• Microsoft founder Bill Gates enjoys a good party. At one of the parties he threw for Microsoft employees, he had six tons of sand brought in, and then he held a contest to see who could build the best sand castle. By the way, Mr. Gates is a billionaire, and he has a mansion that could belong only to a billionaire. It has 40,000 square feet, a garage for 30 cars, video walls that show ever-changing displays of electronic art, a swimming pool with an underwater stereo system, and a room with a 25-foot-high vaulted ceiling to house his trampoline. His "yard" includes a trout stream. Also by the way, two of the world's richest men, Mr. Gates and Warren Buffett, took a two-week trip together through China in October 1995. While riding a train along the Yangtze River, they became engrossed in playing bridge and missed the spectacular scenery until some of their fellow passengers drew their attention to it.[140]

• Early in Charlie Chaplin's career, he was very popular and he wanted to be paid in proportion to his popularity. Essanay Film Company executives were on the verge of giving him a contract for $1,250 per week, but they hesitated because this was a lot of money, especially back then when a usual normal salary was $6 per week. Mr. Chaplin hired a messenger to walk through a hotel where he was meeting with Essanay executives and to call out his name. People passing by, hearing Mr. Chaplin's name, created quite a commotion and quite a crowd, and Mr. Chaplin got his contract. By the way, because Mr. Chaplin was a silent film star early in his career none of his fans knew what he sounded like. Just for the fun of it, he sometimes spoke in a high-pitched squeaky voice to fans who recognized him.[141]

• In the early 1900s in Italy many opera singers were cheated. The impresario of an opera company used to hire people to attend the opera and boo the singer, then the impresario would come backstage and say that because the singer was so unpopular, he was forced to cancel the singer's contract. The impresario would then say that the singer could continue to work if he was willing to sign a new contract for a much lower salary. One impresario tried to play this trick on tenor Enrico Caruso — Mr. Caruso punched him in the face, then left town.[142]

• Major Woodward S. VanDyke II, USMC, was a Hollywood director who knew how to get a bonus. When he directed a movie, he would finish the first print early, in plenty of time to get a bonus for being ahead of schedule, and then he would start doing retakes and really direct his movie. According to actor Sheldon Leonard, "It was not uncommon for VanDyke to take longer on his retakes than on his original production."[143]

• Mark Twain was once down on his luck in San Francisco and almost resorted to begging. Here's how he tells it: "I remember a certain day in San Francisco, when, if I hadn't picked up a dime that I found lying in the street, I should have asked someone for a quarter. Only a matter of a few hours and I'd have been a beggar. That dime saved me, and I have never begged — never."[144]

• British ballerina Violette Verdy was happy when impresario Paul Szilard managed her financial contracts when she worked as director of the Paris Opera Ballet and then as director of the Boston Ballet. She told him, "I am so happy that you are looking after me, because finally I can fly business class, rather than economy."[145]

• Being a stand-up comedian isn't always fun. Once, Carrie Snow was performing at a benefit for charity in a hotel when someone offered to donate $5,000 if she would stop performing. She stopped performing, left the room, and then started crying.[146]

• Jack Benny's comic persona was that of a tightwad. Whenever Rochester, the actor playing his valet, was asked whether Mr. Benny collected anything, he always replied that Mr. Benny had a hobby that kept him very happy — he collected money.[147]

• Comedian Red Skelton was very poor as a child, but very rich as an adult. Frequently, this combination leads to recklessness in personal finance. For example, at one time Mr. Skelton had 200 ties — all the same color (maroon).[148]

Chapter 4: From Mothers to Problem-Solving

Mothers

• Amy Tan, the author of *The Joy Luck Club*, also has a Chinese name, An-mei, which means "blessing from America." Her parents had emigrated from China and had been in the United States for only a short time before having her. Amy's mother, who grew up in China, once told her that she was not affected by World War II, but a few days later, she spoke of running away to get cover from the bombs being dropped from airplanes, adding, "We were always scared that the bombs would fall on top of our heads." When Ms. Tan reminded her mother that she had said that she wasn't affected by the war, she replied, "I wasn't — I wasn't killed."[149]

• Kris Ashman Cypress is very tall, as was her mother. When Kris was a teenager and self-conscious about her height, she asked her mother if she could have an operation to shorten the bones in her arms and legs. Her mother replied, "Yes, but we can only afford to do your legs. So I guess your arms will drag beside you when you walk." Kris writes, "When I finally got the joke, she grabbed me and told me how beautiful I was and how much she loved me. It was her humor and way of looking at life that shocked me out of my teenage bubble of insecurity."[150]

• Alan Bloom scored a major literary success with *The Closing of the American Mind*. Suddenly he had money, and suddenly he began appearing on all the major television shows, including the one hosted by his favorite, Oprah Winfrey. From being a professor, he became a celebrity. When his 90-year-old mother had a stroke, doctors weren't sure about her mental abilities and even whether she would recognize her son. When Mr. Bloom walked into her hospital room, she said, "I know who you are. You wrote *The Closing of the American Mind*."[151]

• "Zora" is the name of a character and a comic strip by lesbian cartoonists Kirsten Zecher and Lori Priestley. In one series of cartoons, Zora's mother, based on the real-life mother of Ms. Zecher, comes out for a visit with her lesbian daughter. Ms. Zecher's mother loved the character based on her, and when the character disappeared in the fourth cartoon of the series, she demanded that they tell her what had happened to the character.[152]

• Ballet mothers help their ballerina daughters in many ways. For example, Eugenia Toumanova, the mother of baby ballerina Tamara Toumanova, used to wear Tamara's new ballet shoes to break them in for her.[153]

Music

• Rhythm and blues superstar Aretha Franklin wears what she likes. Sometimes, she goes to work in a limousine, wearing a mink coat — over top of her T-shirt and jeans. By the way, Aretha often sang one of the Rev. Dr. Martin Luther King's favorite songs, "Precious Lord," for him. The last time Ms. Franklin sang it especially for him was in April of 1968 — at his funeral. Also by the way, Aretha wanted to make sure that blacks heard her music in segregated areas. Therefore, her contract stated that her audiences would always be either integrated or all-black — she declined to perform in front of an all-white audience.[154]

• Oscar Levant went to analysis for years, but he remained an unhappy man. When a friend asked what good psychoanalysis had done for him, Mr. Levant replied, "I'm still unhappy, but at least I have some place to go everyday." Of course, Mr. Levant was known for his morose, grumpy personality. Once, a friend said to him, "Oscar, you sound happy." Mr. Levant replied, "I'm not myself today." By the way, early in his career, Mr. Levant played piano at a little girls' ballet school. He later told his friends, "My work was child's play."[155]

• Tenor Enrico Caruso once seriously studied the flute. A man tried to sell him a new recording machine, and to test the machine, Mr. Caruso played the flute, then listened to the recording. He then asked the salesperson, "Is that how I sound?" The salesperson replied, "Yes, can I sell you the recording machine?" Mr. Caruso said, "No, but I'll sell you the flute."[156]

• Wealthy people sometimes receive insincere praise. Nathan Rothschild, a tremendously wealthy man, once listened to a violinist, then congratulated him on his music. Mr. Rothschild then jingled a few coins in his pocket and said, "That's my music. People listen to it just as carefully. But somehow they don't respect it as much."[157]

• When Sophie Tucker needed an accompanist, she told Ted Shapiro to audition, and if he was good enough, she would give him a contract. Forty years later, Mr. Shapiro was still accompanying Ms. Tucker, and he still didn't have a contract.[158]

Names and Titles

• Stan Freberg's ancestry is Swedish, but despite not being named Johnson, he comes by his name honestly. When his grandfather, Paul Johnson, came to America, the immigration official told him, "What? Not another Johnson? Do you know how many thousands of Swedes I've logged in here with the name of Johnson? Forget it! What don't you change it to something else?" Mr. Johnson thought about what name he wanted the immigration official to put down in writing, and because his mother's name had been Elna Friberg, he spelled her last name for the official, who pronounced it Fry-berg. Mr. Johnson explained that in Swedish the *i* was pronounced *e*, as in Free-burg. The official said, "OK, Freberg," wrote down the name, and the newly named Paul Freberg began life in his new country.[159]

• Balanchine ballerina Allegra Kent was named Iris Margo Cohen when she was born, but anti-Semitism led to the change of her last name. Her mother simply got tired of being turned away by anti-Semitic landlords, and so when Allegra was two years old (she was born in 1937), her mother substituted "Kent" for "Cohen." Her name change from "Iris" to "Allegra" came about because of her sister, who changed her name frequently after becoming sixteen years old. At one point her sister became Wendy Drew — "Wendy" came from *Peter Pan*, and "Drew" came from the Nancy Drew mysteries. Before her sister became Wendy, she made a list of names to choose from. On that list was "Allegra," among other names. Iris liked the name "Allegra" so much that she became Allegra Kent.[160]

• Peter Benchley's first novel was the mega-best seller *Jaws*, which he and his editors had a difficult time naming. They tried out many different titles, and they finally noticed that the only *word* they liked in any of the titles was "jaws." With time running out, they decided to name the novel *Jaws*, a title that really didn't satisfy anyone. According to Mr. Benchley, they felt that "the bottom line was, who cares? Nobody reads first novels anyway." (Mr. Benchley's father, Nathaniel, the son of humorist Robert Benchley, earlier had suggested the title *Who's That Noshin' on My Laig?*)[161]

• The HMS *Beagle* is famous because Charles Darwin sailed on it and collected evidence that supported the theory of evolution. However, the *Beagle* was very small and very crowded — only 90 feet long and with 74 crewmembers. Mr. Darwin's quarters were large in comparison with the quarters of most of the crew, but even he barely had room to turn around. Of course, Mr. Darwin's voyage on the HMS *Beagle* to gather evidence that supported the theory of evolution is well known. Less well known is that British sailors referred to the *Beagle* and ships of its type as "coffins," because of their unfortunate tendency, during bad weather, to sink.[162]

• Before becoming a famous comedian, Sid Caesar was a jazz saxophonist. He played with Gene Krupa's band, along with pianist Teddy Napoleon and Teddy's sister, Josephine, who was the vocalist. One day, Sid, Teddy, and Josephine were driving to a gig, and a police officer stopped them. Teddy was driving, so the police officer looked at his driver's license. He was amused by Teddy's last name, Napoleon, and Sid laughed and said that his name was Caesar. The police officer looked at the only woman in the car and said, "And I suppose you're Josephine." Teddy's sister replied, "Yes, how did you know?"[163]

• After leaving prison, Oscar Wilde went to France, where he stayed at the Hotel Sandwich. Two friends, Robert Ross and Reginald Turner, also stayed with him. Mr. Wilde was widely hated at this time, so he stayed at the hotel under an assumed name, and he wrote a friend that Robert Ross was staying at the hotel under the name of Reginald Turner, and Reginald Turner was staying at the hotel under the name of Robert Ross, because "it is better that they should not use their own names."[164]

• When Steve Wozniak was married to Candi Clark, they had a son they named "Jesse John Clark." They decided to use Candi's last name because "Wozniak" is difficult to spell. As a co-founder of the Apple Computer Company, Mr. Wozniak made millions, so he had money to play with. When he built a house, he designed part of it to look like a limestone cave — complete with fake cave wall paintings, fossils, and dinosaur footprints.[165]

• When Rudolf Bing became general manager of the Metropolitan Opera, his appointment was kept secret for a while. When he went to a photographer to have his portrait taken to accompany the press release that would announce his appointment, he used an assumed name. When the assumed name was called, he failed to stand up — because he had forgotten the name.[166]

• Alan Brady's original name on the pilot that became the basis of *The Dick Van Dyke Show* was Alan Sturdy, chosen by creator Carl Reiner because it sounded strong. The name was changed because executive producer Sheldon Leonard and comedian Morey Amsterdam (who played Buddy Sorrell) both thought the name sounded like "Alan's Dirty."[167]

• When he was a youth (and later), choreographer George Balanchine had a habitual sniff or facial tic that made him bare his front teeth. Other dance students noticed this, and they gave him a nickname: Rat.[168]

• Count Basie got his name early in his career, when he was often late for rehearsals. Frequently, the bandleader Bennie Moten would look around, see that Mr. Basie was not present, then shout, "Where is that no-'count Basie?"[169]

• A homophobe once said to lesbian comedian Robin Tyler, "They should take all the homosexuals and put them on an island." Ms. Tyler replied, "They did, and they call it Manhattan."[170]

Opera

• African-American diva Shirley Verrett learned a lot from performing various roles in opera. She debuted in opera in 1957 playing the title role in *The Rape of Lucretia* by Benjamin Britten, and in 1958 she played Irina in *Lost in the Stars* by Kurt Weill. She once said, "That showed me how I could change characters, being a virgin one night and two nights later a dance hall girl coming down the stairs with a split in my skirt. Everything I had learned in church went right down the drain!"[171]

• During a performance of *Lohengrin*, tenor Leo Slezak still had not met the woman playing Elsa of Brabant. During the performance, following the script, he said, "Elsa, I love thee," and raised her from her kneeling position and placed her head against his chest, then whispered, "Allow me to introduce myself; my name is Slezak." The woman playing Elsa then whispered in reply, "Delighted to know you; my name is Ternina."[172]

• In Giacomo Puccini's opera *Tosca*, the title character commits suicide by jumping off the ramparts of the Castel Sant' Angelo in Rome into the Tiber River. Mr. Puccini pointed out to the author of the original play, Victorien Sardou, that the river is too far from the castle for this to happen, but Mr. Sardou told him not to worry about such a minor point.[173]

Parties

• Sometimes, young people don't appreciate when they are surrounded by genius — although they do appreciate it later. Felia Doubrovska danced in Sergei Diaghilev's ballet company, where she worked with and was surrounded by people such as Bronislavka Nijinsky, George Balanchine, Pablo Picasso, Jean Cocteau, Georges Auric, and Sergei Prokofiev. At a party thrown by Coco Chanel, Igor Stravinsky was playing the piano, and Mr. Diaghilev told Ms. Doubrovska, "Eat later. Now listen and try to learn something." Mr. Stravinsky was playing *Les Noces* — in the ballet of which Ms. Doubrovska later danced the role of the Bride.[174]

• Joseph Chamberlain was the after-dinner speaker at a party where the guests were enjoying themselves very much. When the time for his speech approached, he was asked, "Shall we let these people enjoy themselves a little longer, or will you give your speech now?"[175]

Poetry and Poets

• Maxwell Bodenheim considered himself the 376th ranking poet in the United States because he had entered 376 poetry contests and had never won a prize. By the way, Ben Hecht once said, "One of the happiest failures of civilization is that it has never been able to kill off the poets. It tries hard by ignoring and starving them. Luckily the poets have always been able to survive. It is the voice of the poets, more than the historians, that tells us who and what we are."[176]

• While at Trinity College, Dublin, Oscar Wilde read a poem, causing the class bully to sneer. This made Mr. Wilde angry, so he asked the bully to explain himself. Once again, the bully sneered. To settle the dispute, the two decided to fight. No one gave Wilde, who avoided competitive sports, a chance, but he soundly beat up the bully.[177]

Practical Jokes

• Opera singers constantly worry about catching colds. Tenor Leo Slezak knew a baritone at the Vienna Opera who was especially worried. To prevent this disaster from occurring, he wore large cotton earplugs, taking them out for rehearsals and to perform, but leaving them in his ears while on the street. The baritone once sang the role of John the Baptist in Richard Strauss' *Salome*. In this opera, John's head is carried onstage on a silver platter, covered with a cloth. For one performance, Mr. Slezak secretly made a few modifications to the papier-mâché head of John the Baptist — when the cloth was removed onstage, the head was wearing two large cotton earplugs.[178]

• While Eve Arden was appearing in a play, Tallulah Bankhead and her date watched from the audience and tried to break up the cast with laughter. Her date was wearing a wide red ribbon across his chest. At a crucial moment in the play, white lights shone in the ribbon, spelling out the words, "Call for Phillip Morris," the slogan of the sponsor of Tallulah's radio show.[179]

• A man died, leaving behind a will that stated that in a certain closet was a sealed box. The will gave the strictest order that the box must not be opened, but must be burned until it was nothing but ashes. The man's sons and daughters carried out his wishes — only to learn that the box was filled with firecrackers.[180]

• Wilson Mizner was a card sharp, and he knew a lot of other gamblers who were also card sharps. Once, he brought a deck of cards consisting of all aces to a card game, and after dealing a hand from the deck, he watched with amusement as all the other players attempted to get rid of their extra ace.[181]

Prejudice

• Back in the Jim Crow days when African-Americans were forced to sit at the back of the bus, black comedian Dick Gregory used to do a routine about the first black bus driver in the Jim Crow South: "Can you imagine how it will be, when they hire the first Negro bus driver in the South, and the steering wheel's 25 feet long?" He also joked, "What a country! Where else could I have to ride in the back of the bus, live in the worst neighborhoods, go to the worst schools, eat in the worst restaurants — and average $5,000 a week just talking about it?"[182]

• In 1936, the Nazis invited modern dance pioneer Martha Graham to perform at the International Dance Festival, an event they were holding in conjunction with the Olympic Games. She declined, pointing out that many members of her dance company were Jewish and that she would not dance in a country that persecuted Jews. After World War II was over, Ms. Graham's name appeared on a list of people the Nazis were going to "take care of" once they had conquered the United States.[183]

• Many teenagers, and especially gay teenagers, have a difficult time in high school. After high school, a gay man attended a Forgiveness Workshop, where he was told to bring photographs of the people who had hurt him in his youth so that he could throw the photographs into a pink, heart-shaped wastebasket. The gay man threw his high school yearbook into the wastebasket.[184]

• Bert Williams was a famous black comedian who performed in the Ziegfeld Follies early in the 20th century. While touring in a southern city, Mr. Williams walked into a bar and ordered a drink. The bartender said, "OK, but it will cost you $50." Mr. Williams reached into his pocket, took out three $100 bills, laid them on the bar, and said, "I'll take six."[185]

Problem-Solving

• Michael Wigge, a German television personality, is able to come up with good ways to make money when needed. In San Francisco, California, he wanted to raise money so that he could fly to Costa Rica. He raised the necessary $300 with pillows. He says, "I took two pillows from my couch-surfing hosts and offered pillow fighting to passersby for a little donation. San Franciscans really seem to be in need of a good pillow fight. A young man in Dolores Park took a pillow and hit me in my face as hard as he could — I didn't even have a chance to fight back. Two businessmen opted to fight each other on their lunch break and gave me $20 to stay out of it. People started queuing up in Golden Gate Park to take part." This worked: He raised enough money to fly to Costa Rica. Other ways that he has raised money to fund his travel is by acting as a human sofa: He gets on all fours and lets people sit on him and catch their breath. His sign said, "Relax for one dollar by sitting on the human sofa!" In addition, he has worked as a hill helper. San Francisco has steep hills, and he helps people climb up hills. He says, "As the Hill Helper, I pushed groaning tourists up the incline [of Lombard Street] by holding their back with my hands. They leaned back and put their entire weight on my hands to be pushed uphill. It was real backbreaking work (my back, not theirs)."[186]

• Early in Marilyn Monroe's career, when she was a model, a photographer told her that her nose was too long. Emmeline Snively, owner of the Blue Book Agency, examined Ms. Monroe's face and told her that she needed more space between her nose and her upper lip. One way to solve the problem would be to develop a new smile — one in which as she smiled she pulled down on her upper lip. Ms. Monroe developed the new smile, but the effort of smiling in this way made her lips tremble. By the way, in 1953, both Ms. Monroe and Jane Russell, co-stars of *Gentlemen Prefer Blondes*, had the honor of being immortalized outside Grauman's Chinese Theater by putting their handprints and writing their autographs in wet cement. Ms. Monroe signed her name, then dotted the "i" in "Marilyn" with a rhinestone in honor of her song "Diamonds are a Girl's Best Friend." Unfortunately, a souvenir seeker quickly stole the rhinestone.[187]

• Screenwriters Ben Hecht and Charlie MacArthur once had a hard time dealing with their mail — reading and answering it took too much time away from their work. Finally, they found a way to solve their problem. They hired someone to dump their mail — still unopened — into the fireplace each morning. By the way, Mr. Hecht once said, "A town without a newspaper is a dead town. Without newspapers, without their daffy headlines, their pontificators and buzzing columnists and pictures to look at, a town loses its identity. You don't realize how important papers are when they're rolling off the presses, but when the presses stop, you feel Scheherazade has left town. One can't help but yearn for the fellow who writes the daily mad-hatter drama of the town, Mr. Journalism."[188]

• Making maps in ancient times was very difficult. To measure the distances between two points, map makers hired professional walkers — people who had been trained to take steps of the same distance, instead of mixing up long and short steps. The professional walkers would walk the distance between two points, then report to the map maker how many steps they had taken. The ancient Greek mathematician and scientist Eratosthenes hired a professional walker to measure the distance between Alexandria and Syene, then he used the measurement to calculate the circumference of the Earth. He came up with the figure of 29,000 miles, which is close to the actual figure of approximately 24,900 miles.[189]

• The movie *Field of Dreams* starred Kevin Costner as a man who builds a baseball field in his cornfield. Of course, the movie had to be carefully planned so that the corn would be the right height when the time for filming the scenes in the cornfield came. The corn was planted, and the director filmed the indoor scenes first to allow time for the corn to grow. Unfortunately, because of a drought it seemed that the corn would not grow after all. However, the creators of the film dammed a creek and irrigated the field, and they even paid $25,000 to truck in water. This was so successful that Mr. Costner sometimes had to walk on hidden platforms in the cornfield because the corn was so high.[190]

• Girls at a middle school started to wear lipstick. Unfortunately, this caused a problem. They would put the lipstick on in the girls' restroom and then kiss the mirror, leaving behind lipstick on the mirror. The principal decided to get the girls to stop doing that. She called all the girls into the bathroom and explained, "The lipstick on the mirror is very difficult for the janitor to get off." The principal then asked the janitor, "Will you please show the girls how difficult it is for you to get the lipstick off the mirror?" The janitor dipped a toilet brush into the water in a toilet and then used the brush to scrub the mirror. The girls stopped kissing the mirror.[191]

• While on tour with the Mapleson Opera Company, Etelka Gerster became stubborn after her sleeping car broke down, and the train stopped so that the broken car could be put on a side rail. Against all reason, Ms. Gerster absolutely refused to leave the sleeping car. Fortunately, Colonel James H. Mapleson solved the problem by convincing a very handsome station agent to play the role of the president of the railroad. The station agent flattered the stubborn coloratura, then convinced her to travel in another sleeping car that he said had been prepared especially for her.[192]

• When writers Ben Hecht and Charles MacArthur ran a movie studio that produced their own scripts in the 1930s, they hired a stage actor named Claude Rains to appear before a movie camera for the first time in their movie *Crime Without Passion*. Because he had a problem with his feet swelling under the hot movie lights, Mr. Rains performed many of his love scenes while standing barefoot in a pan of cool water — the movie camera, of course, was kept focused above his waist.[193]

• Edwin Booth and Tommaso Salvini appeared together in *Othello* over a century ago. Mr. Booth appeared as Iago, and Mr. Salvini appeared as Othello. Mr. Booth performed well in the early acts, but he became ill and could barely stand when Othello assaulted him. He nearly fell into the orchestra pit, but Mr. Salvini used his immense strength to hold him up and continued to perform the scene as if Mr. Booth were not ill.[194]

• As a computer pioneer, Grace Hopper thought in original ways. Frequently, after she was told that a problem could not be solved, she went ahead and tried to solve it anyway. She explained, "It's much easier to apologize than it is to get permission." She also owned a clock that ran counter-clockwise simply to show people that things can be done in more than the usual way.[195]

• Lord Berkeley often boasted that he would never be robbed by a lone highwayman. One night, he was accosted by a lone highwayman, so Lord Berkeley, thinking quickly, said, "You cowardly dog, do you think that I can't see your confederate skulking behind you?" The highwayman turned around to look — and Lord Berkeley shot him.[196]

• Actress Madge Titheradge had a reputation for fainting unnecessarily. In *Theater Royal*, she fainted at the end of the second act. Actress Dame Marie Tempest saw her fall; not being in a mood to tolerate such foolishness, she raised a stick that was part of her costume and was about to hit her — but Ms. Titheradge made a sudden recovery and picked herself off the floor.[197]

• Stand-up comedian Steve Mittleman found an original way to handle a heckler at the Comedy Store. He said, "Sir, I just want to share the fact that I really love you and care about you." This was not the reaction the heckler had expected, so he kept quiet after that.[198]

• While traveling overseas to perform his magic act, Harry Kellar faced the problem of how to hide his money so it would not be stolen. To solve the problem, he used to hide his gold coins in cans of sticky black material that was used to pave roads.[199]

Chapter 5: From Puns and Word Play to Work

Puns and Word Play

• At one time, Rachel Heyhoe Flint was the captain of the England women's cricket team. In a store, she saw a package of frozen custard bearing the label, "Makes a pie for four people, or 12 little tarts." She said, "I hadn't realized that it would be such a good opportunity to invite the current England women's cricket team."[200]

• Thomas De Quincey once attended a dinner party where an old woman talked on and on. His hostess apologized to him later, saying of the old woman, "She's practically in her dotage." Mr. De Quincey replied, "I would call it anecdotage."[201]

Religion

• Ted Shawn was thinking about creating a solo dance using as inspiration the Hindu god Siva, the destroyer. Thinking that he had taken on a huge task, he told a disciple of the Vedanta cult, named Boshi Sen, "What an awful fool I've been. Who am I that I should dare this task that's beyond human doing?" Boshi Sen replied, "You don't have to do it. Make your body an instrument and remove your petty self from it, and Siva will use your body to dance through. You will not be dancing, you, the little personal Ted Shawn, but Siva will dance — if you ask him to." Mr. Shawn did precisely that — after he had choreographed the dance, each time he performed it he asked Siva to take over his body and use it to express Siva's own being. Mr. Shawn said, "The dance never failed to reach its audience with its power."[202]

• Some people have a gift for discovering the fossils of dinosaurs. One group of fossil hunters at a quarry were having very little luck finding fossils, but when Robert Bakker arrived there, he quickly discovered a jawbone and other fossils. Mr. Bakker said, "They thought I belonged to a secret religion."[203]

Royalty

• Following a concert in Manchester, Sir Thomas Beecham saw a woman he realized that he had met before, although he couldn't remember where and he couldn't remember who she was. Unable to get past her without her seeing him, he remembered that she had a brother, and so he went to the woman and asked about her brother and whether or not he still had the same job. The woman replied, "He is very well — and he is still King."[204]

• A ruler pretended to dislike flattery, but one of his subordinates knew that the ruler really liked flattery, so he told the ruler, "All of the other rulers like flattery — you are the only ruler who dislikes it." The ruler, pleased, asked, "How did you know that I dislike flattery?"[205]

Scientists and Science

• At the South Pole, the temperature has been measured as low as minus 117 degrees Fahrenheit. How cold is that? If you were to take a glass of water and throw the water into the air, it would turn to ice before it hit the ground. Living in very cold environments requires adjustments: 1) Batteries don't work at very low temperatures, so scientists at the South Pole use solar energy to power their Walkmans when they can, but during the long Antarctic night, they use a frying pan to carefully heat up batteries so they will work. 2) At the Amundsen-Scott South Pole Station, located at the South Pole, food is kept in a walk-in refrigerator. Unlike ordinary refrigerators, however, the South Pole refrigerator is kept heated so that the food doesn't freeze. 3) Researchers and animals at Antarctica eat high-calorie, high-fat diets — simply keeping one's body warm requires a huge number of calories. The milk that Weddell seal pups drink contains about 20 times the fat of the milk that comes from cows. (Weddell seals are interesting animals — because they can store huge amounts of oxygen in their blood and muscles, they can swim under the Antarctic ice for close to an hour without taking a breath.) 4) Life can be tenacious. At Antarctica, where the environment is brutal, lichens live just *underneath* the surface of rocks. By the way, on Antarctica is an aquarium used for the purpose of studying Antarctic cod. A sign by the aquarium says, "Experiment in Progress. Do Not Feed, Pinch, Fondle, or Kiss the Fish." This is good advice, as the mouth of the Antarctic cod is so large that it could easily bite someone's hand off.[206]

• Anton Mesmer invented mesmerism, based on the idea that people had animal magnetism, and that people could pass this animal magnetism from one person to another person. People who thought they had been magnetized did odd things, and some people who were ill claimed to feel better after being magnetized. In 1784, Antoine Lavoisier, the founder of modern chemistry, and some other scientists investigated animal magnetism. In one experiment, the scientists blindfolded people and told them that Mr. Mesmer was present and was magnetizing them. The people, who did not know that Mr. Mesmer was not present and was not trying to magnetize them, acted oddly. In another experiment, Mr. Mesmer hid behind a screen and tried to magnetize people. The people, who did not know that Mr. Mesmer was behind the screen and was trying to magnetize them, acted normally. As a result of their investigation, Mr. Lavoisier and the other scientists concluded that animal magnetism did not exist.[207]

• As a young man, Charles Darwin was a collector of zoological specimens, including beetles. Once he found three rare specimens of beetles at the same time. Not wanting to lose any of the specimens, he carried a beetle in each of his hands, and he put the third beetle in his mouth. Unfortunately, the beetle sprayed a liquid that burned his mouth so badly that he spit the beetle out. Of course, during his voyage on the HMS *Beagle*, Mr. Darwin spent a great deal of time on land, where he collected zoological and botanical specimens. Each time he saw a new species of animal, he shot it and shipped it back to England to be studied by specialists. In a single day, Mr. Darwin once collected 68 new beetle species, and during a single morning walk, he once shot 80 different bird species. Sailors on the *Beagle* called him "the

Flycatcher" and joked that he wanted to collect all of South American animal and plant life and send it to England in specimen jars.[208]

• As a mathematics professor at Princeton, John von Neumann acquired a reputation among his students for writing numbers on the board and then erasing them before the students were able to copy them. He was also known for driving poorly. In fact, he had so many auto accidents at one particular corner that it became informally known as the "Von Neumann Corner." Mr. von Neumann worked on the Manhattan Project at Los Alamos, New Mexico, and helped develop the atomic bomb. Later, he worked for the Atomic Energy Commission. When he was dying of cancer, he had to take heavy dosages of medicine. The government made sure that the people taking care of him all had security clearances just in case he accidentally let secrets slip while under the medication.[209]

• Edward Hitchcock was the first American to study dinosaur fossils, although he did not realize what the fossils were — the study of dinosaurs was still in its infancy then. Even as a teenager, Mr. Hitchcock demonstrated his high intelligence. A publisher once offered a prize to anyone who discovered any mathematical errors in a new nautical almanac. After young Mr. Hitchcock discovered 80 errors in the almanac, the publisher withdrew the offer of the prize.[210]

• When astronomer Carl Sagan was a boy, he went to the library and asked for a book about stars — the librarian handed him a book about movie stars. After young Carl had explained what he wanted in more detail, the librarian showed him the library section devoted to astronomy.[211]

Television

• The Simpsons live in Springfield, but in what state? Springfield, Ohio? Springfield, Oregon? Springfield, Massachusetts? Springfield, wherever? In one episode, Marge is talking on the telephone and saying where she lives when Homer walks in: "Springfield, Oh hi ya, Homer." In the May 2012 issue of *Smithsonian Magazine*, *Simpsons* creators

Matt Groening talked about the Simpsons' Springfield: "Springfield was named after Springfield, Oregon. The only reason is that when I was a kid, the TV show *Father Knows Best* took place in the town of Springfield, and I was thrilled because I imagined that it was the town next to Portland, my hometown. When I grew up, I realized it was just a fictitious name. I also figured out that Springfield was one of the most common names for a city in the U.S. In anticipation of the success of the show, I thought, 'This will be cool; everyone will think it's their Springfield.' And they do." Over the years, he has been kind to people who want to believe that Springfield is in their state. He said, "I don't want to ruin it for people, you know? Whenever people say it's Springfield, Ohio, or Springfield, Massachusetts, or Springfield, wherever, I always go, 'Yup, that's right.'"[212]

• The *Star Trek* actors who played James Tiberius Kirk and Mister Spock, William Shatner and Leonard Nimoy, are both Jewish. In fact, the famous Vulcan hand greeting with thumb stretched wide, the index and middle fingers together, and the ring and pinkie fingers together, comes from a priestly blessing of ancient Jerusalem and is still used in some present-day Jewish congregations.[213]

• While on *The Tonight Show*, starring Johnny Carson, fashion designer Oleg Cassini described one of his dresses in this way: "This is a lovely hostess dinner dress with a very low neckline for easy entertaining." By the way, when Johnny Carson learned that one of his TV guests had had twins, he said, "That's about the greatest labor-saving device in the world."[214]

• Comedian Lucille Ball once appeared on an TV show called *The Virginia Graham Show*. A second guest was a magician who used balls in his sleight-of-hand tricks. While demonstrating his tricks, he asked Lucy, "You think I have two balls?" Lucy replied, "I hope so."[215]

Theater

• *My Fair Lady* was a major hit on Broadway and tickets were very difficult to buy. One lady and her husband showed up at the ticket office and were forced to admit that they had mislaid their tickets; however, they did have the stub of the check which they had used to pay for the tickets, and they did have the numbers of the tickets written down on the check stubs. The theater manager showed the couple to the orchestra stall, where they discovered their next-door neighbors sitting in the seats they had purchased tickets for. Astonished, the woman asked, "How did you get those seats?" The next-door neighbors explained, "Your daughter sold the tickets to us."[216]

• As a young man, L. Frank Baum, who later wrote *The Wonderful Wizard of Oz*, formed a Shakespearean troupe. One review of the troupe's *Hamlet* stated, "The only successful performance occurred when the ghost of Hamlet's father fell through a hole in the stage. The audience, which happened to be composed of oil workers, was so delighted that the unhappy ghost had to repeat the stunt five times." By the way, on 16 June 1902, a theatrical version of *The Wonderful Wizard of Oz* opened. In the beginning part of his performance as the Scarecrow, Fred Stone was required to sit on stage motionless on stage for 18 minutes.[217]

• Eve Arden was getting ready to go on stage in Los Angeles, California, in the title role of *Auntie Mame* when she realized she couldn't remember the name of the Connecticut town where Mame's nephew's snooty fiancé lived. She turned to a cast member who played one of the Connecticut group and asked, "Quick, Frank, where do you live?" Misunderstanding her, he told her the name of his Los Angeles hotel. Fortunately, Ms. Arden remembered the name of the Connecticut town once she was onstage.[218]

• Robert Benchley and Dorothy Parker got to know playwright Robert E. Sherwood (later to become twice a Pulitzer Prize-winner for *Idiot's Delight* and *Abe Lincoln in Illinois*) because he asked to go to lunch with them — and to walk between them. They soon found out why. Mr. Sherwood was six-feet-seven, and some little people near where he worked used to lie in wait for him and walk him to his restaurant while shouting things like "How's the weather up there?"[219]

• Dame Edith Evans consistently made the same mistake during rehearsals for *Hay Fever*, saying, "On a very clear day you can see Marlow." Mr. Coward told her, "Dear Edith, you spoil the rhythm by putting in a 'very.' The line is 'On a clear morning you can see Marlow.' On a very clear morning you can also see both Beaumont and Fletcher."[220]

• Shakespeare was very popular in Yiddish translations in Yiddish theaters. Once, a Yiddish-speaking taxi driver asked Walter Matthau what he was doing. Mr. Matthau replied that he was performing in a Broadway production of *King Lear*. The taxi driver replied, "Really? Do you think it would go in English?"[221]

• While performing in a Marx Brothers play on Broadway, Groucho went to the footlights and asked, "Is there a doctor in the house?" When a doctor stood up, Groucho asked him, "If you're a doctor, why aren't you at the hospital making your patients miserable, instead of wasting your time here with that blonde?"[222]

Travel

• Balletomanes sometimes think that the life of ballet dancers and choreographers is glamorous, but it often isn't. Early in ballerina Maria Tallchief's career, she and other lowly paid ballet dancers often played "Ghosting," aka "That Old Army Game." One dancer would rent a room, then two other dancers would sneak in and stay there, too. One dancer would sleep on the bed, another on the box springs, and a third on the floor. Because of wartime conditions, however, rooms were not always available, and Ms. Tallchief once saw famed choreographer Agnes de Mille sleeping on a table in a hotel hallway.[223]

• Estimating travel times accurately used to be very difficult, as naturalist Charles Darwin found out when he set sail on the *Beagle*. Robert FitzRoy, Captain of the *Beagle*, thought that the voyage would take two years. The actual time it took for the *Beagle* to return home again was five years! By the way, when Mr. Darwin wished to learn how to stuff birds, his teacher was a black man named John Edmonstone, who had been a slave in South America but was freed.[224]

• When Oscar Wilde arrived in the United States for his 1882 lecture tour, he went through customs, where he stated, "I have nothing to declare but my genius." By the way, during his American lecture tour, Oscar Wilde was asked whether he had in fact walked with a lily in his hand down Piccadilly — as legend had it. Mr. Wilde replied, "To have done it was nothing, but to make people think one had done it was a triumph."[225]

• Melissa Hayden, a ballerina with the New York City Ballet, used to travel with a special circular bag which held a flattened tutu. Stewardesses often wondered what was in it, and Billy Weslow, a funny but sometimes crude NYCB dancer, often yelled, "It's her diaphragm!"[226]

War

• After unsuccessfully trying to capture Pancho Villa in Mexico, Charles MacArthur and his military outfit returned to America, where they were given a parade in which a drunken Mr. MacArthur steered a car down the street with one hand while he waved an American flag with the other. As he drove, he shouted anti-military slogans such as "Down with Colonel Foreman" — Colonel Milton Foreman was his commanding officer. Mr. MacArthur was punished by being forced to pick up litter at the military base. Because he found that boring, he made some alterations to his blue prisoner suit. He used gold radiator paint for stripes, added epaulets and other decorations, and succeeded so well that visitors to the base thought he was a general — but an oddly acting general, since he saluted each piece of litter before picking it up. Colonel Foreman saw him and gave him his discharge papers that same day. Years later, Mr. MacArthur, then a famous playwright, and his wife, the famous actress Helen Hayes, saw Colonel Foreman and introduced themselves to him. According to Ms. Hayes, as soon as the colonel heard Mr. MacArthur's name and remembered who he was, "The colonel's face turned slowly purple, and his eyes seemed to go out of focus. Then, without saying a word, he stood up and stalked away."[227]

• John Glenn was one of the first seven astronauts chosen to participate in the United States' space program. At a news conference, a reporter asked the seven Mercury astronauts to raise their hands if they felt that they could go into space then return to Earth safely. All of the astronauts raised a hand in the air except for Mr. Glenn — who raised both of his hands in the air. By the way, during the Korean War, Mr. Glenn, a pilot, was anxious to fight some Russian-made MiGs. Because of Mr. Glenn's eagerness, the squadron artist painted on the side of Mr. Glenn's plane the legend "MIG MAD MARINE." Eventually, Mr. Glenn got his wish — in nine days, he shot down three MiGs. Also by the way, after Mr. Glenn had become the first American to orbit the earth, he went back to his hometown of New Concord, Ohio, to star in a parade. Although New Concord had a population of only 2,100, more than 40,000 people lined its streets to watch the parade.[228]

• Harold Ross believed in separating the editorial staff and the advertising staff of *The New Yorker* — he put the departments in two separate buildings two blocks apart. By the way, during World War II, when England was constantly being bombed by the Germans, *New Yorker* writer James Thurber underwent a series of eye operations. Mr. Ross visited him at the hospital and told him, "Damn it, Thurber, I worry about you and England."[229]

Wit

• Hollywood is filled with witty people: 1) A publicist once wired Cary Grant's agent, "How old Cary Grant?" However, Mr. Grant saw the message, and he wired the publicist back, "Old Cary Grant fine. How you?" 2) Woody Allen says he decided to name a movie of his *Bananas* "because there are no bananas in it." 3) When Cinemascope — which widened the movie screen in an attempt to compete with television — first appeared, some Hollywood talents opposed it. According to George Stevens (director of *Shane* and *I Remember Mama*), "It's fine if you want a system that shows a boa constrictor to better advantage than a man." 4) Marlon Brando once observed something strange about being a movie star: "Once you are a star actor, people start asking you questions about politics, astronomy, archaeology, and birth control." 5) Julie Andrews' first movie was Disney's *Mary Poppins*, for which she won an Oscar. Some people believed that she won because the voters felt sympathy for her because Warner Brothers had not let her star in the movie version of *My Fair Lady*, in which she had starred on stage. When Ms. Andrews received the Oscar, she said in her acceptance speech, "I'd like to thank all those who made this possible — especially Jack Warner."[230]

******

• Wilson Mizner was a great scoundrel and a great wit: 1) During a hard winter in New York, when con men were preying on each other, Mr. Mizner recommended that con men wear roses in the lapels of their coats so they could be identified by other con men. 2) Mizner once read a story to Jim Tully, who liked the story so much he wired an editor, who immediately offered $1,000 for it. Mr. Mizner complained, "It took me over eight hours to write that." 3) Mr. Mizner was with fighter-author Jim Tully when Mr. Tully's secretary gave him the news that Calvin Coolidge, who was noted for seldom speaking, had died. Without even looking up, Mr. Mizner asked, "How can they tell?" 4) Mr. Mizner was once told by his host to leave the house. He replied, "A gentleman never leaves a house until told to do so by a gentleman." 5) Mizner liked to get up late in the afternoon — he often boasted that he had never seen a sunrise.[231]

   • Three short witty anecdotes: 1) Hillaire Belloc could be very imposing. He once arrived late at a lecture he was giving, but told everyone present, "I am half an hour late. It is entirely my fault. I do not apologize." 2) At the end of their career, authors sometimes publish a collection of their writing and title it *The Works of* .... However, *The Works of Max Beerbohm* appeared when Max was all of 23 years old. 3) James McNeill Whistler, the famous painter, was once asked, "Do you think genius is hereditary?" He replied, "I can't tell you; heaven has granted me no offspring."[232]

• Actor Peter Ustinov had a cigarette in his mouth when director Fred Zinnemann told him, "You can't concentrate with a cigarette in your mouth." Mr. Ustinov replied, "You mean, you can't concentrate with a cigarette in my mouth." By the way, Mr. Ustinov received very poor critical notices for his play *No Sign of the Dove*. According to Sir Peter, "Yes, I had to fight like a stag to get the critics to attack me." Also by the way, Mr. Ustinov's preferred way of shutting up bores is to say to them, "Now, Singapore — does that mean anything to you?"[233]

• Prime Minister David Lloyd George was a small man. At a political meeting, he was once introduced in this way: "I had expected to see Mr. Lloyd George a big man in every sense, but you see for yourself he is quite small in stature." Mr. Lloyd George replied, "In North Wales we measure a man from the chin up. You evidently measure from the chin down."[234]

• In the 18th century, Richard Porson was Regius Professor of Greek at Cambridge University. He had a number of enemies, one of whom told him, "Dr. Porson, my opinion of you is most contemptible." Dr. Porson replied, "Sir, I never knew an opinion of yours that was not contemptible."[235]

• Society lady Helen Choate Bell of Boston disliked the great outdoors. Hearing that some friends were going to spend a day in the woods, she said, "Kick a tree for me." She was also against automobiles, saying that they would divide Humankind into two groups: the quick and the dead.[236]

• Critics denounced Arthur Wood's performance as Bottom in Shakespeare's *Midsummer's Night Dream*, so Mr. Wood wrote an angry letter to a newspaper. The editor printed the letter, but added this note: "Mr. Wood seems rather thin-skinned about his Bottom."[237]

Work

• Singer/songwriter Jack White used to make a living as an upholsterer. As you may expect, he was an unusual upholsterer. Everything in his business — clothing, tools, even his van — had to be yellow or white or black. Why? He explained that it was "an aesthetic presentation." When he made out his bills, he used crayon. When he restored furniture, he hid in the upholstery poems for the next upholsterer who would restore the furniture. Mr. White said, "I thought, we're the only ones to see inside this furniture, we should be talking to each other, like the Egyptian masons might leave a message on the stone they were putting in the pyramid." He even formed a band with another upholsterer. The band, obviously, was called the Upholsterers. They recorded a single, made 100 copies, and hid them inside the furniture they restored. Mr. White said, "Not one's been found yet. They were on clear vinyl with transparency covers, so even if you x-rayed the furniture, you wouldn't be able to find them. I know where a couple of them might be, but it's very funny in that sense."[238]

• During the Alaskan gold rush, some people made lots of money serving as goldweighers in cafés and saloons. Miners came into various places of business and paid for their purchases in gold. One goldweigher grew long fingernails so he could secrete some gold dust under his fingernails during each transaction. Another goldweigher wore his hair long and well oiled, and he ran his fingers often through his hair — at the end of the day he would give himself a shampoo and collect the gold dust from the bottom of the basin. For a while, Wilson Mizner worked as a goldweigher. He used to spill some gold dust on the square of carpet under his feet — at the end of the day he would burn the square of carpet and collect the gold dust from the ashes. Mr. Mizner later boasted, "I weighed a million and a half dollars' worth of gold dust at Swiftwater Bill's joint, and never made a mistake that wasn't in favor of the house."[239]

• An early performance of Peter Ustinov's *Love of Four Colonels* ran for four hours, so of course Mr. Ustinov was told to cut 90 minutes from his play. He replied, "Why? *Hamlet* ran for four hours — and this play's much funnier." By the way, anyone who works with other people will have occasional problems. Mr. Ustinov once said that he thought Walt Disney must have been happy while making an animated film: "If one of his characters became difficult, all he had to do was to erase it." Also by the way, Mr. Ustinov has a boat, about which he says: "It can sleep six people who know each other very well. Or one prude."[240]

• Microsoft founder Bill Gates knows how to express his opinion. More than one Microsoft computer programmer has received an e-mail from Mr. Gates stating, "This is the stupidest piece of code ever written." Mr. Gates has the credibility to get away with his bluntness — in addition to being the billionaire owner of Microsoft, he scored a perfect 800 on the math portion of his Scholastic Aptitude Test. Microsoft computer programmers worked long, hard hours, but they did have special amusements provided for them, including a room set aside specially for juggling.[241]

• For a while, Amy Tan, author of *The Joy Luck Club*, worked 80- and 90-hour weeks as a freelance technical writer. Eventually, she went to a therapist, but she soon quit because he kept falling asleep during their sessions. Especially upsetting her was that the therapist fell asleep only when she talked about good things; whenever she talked about bad things, he was extremely attentive. This, she felt, reinforced her negative feelings and was a second good reason to stop seeing the therapist.[242]

• When Count Basie broke up his big band and started a sextet, everyone was surprised that Freddie "Pepper" Green, an important part of Count Basie's "All-American Rhythm Section" for 14 years, was not part of the sextet. But Pepper showed up for work anyway, telling Count Basie, "After I gave you the best years of my life, you think you're going to leave me now?" The six-musician group became a seven-musician group, and Pepper worked for Count Basie another 35 years.[243]

• The Marx Brothers once ordered their writers to show up at 9:30 a.m. for a meeting. The writers pointed out that they were always at work by 9:30, so Groucho responded, "Well, then, come in at 8:30." The writers did come in at 8:30, but the Marx Brothers didn't show up until 11:45. The writers complained, "Where were you? We were right here!" Groucho said, "How do you like that? They were right here. We go out of our way to have a meeting and they just sit here!"[244]

• Heinrich Conried, director of the Metropolitan Opera in New York City, knew that the clouds in Wagner's *Walküre* are important, and once he spent three hours rehearsing the movement of the clouds with the stagehands before a performance. He then told them, "Very good! If you do it as well as that tonight, I shall be much pleased." One of the stagehands replied, "But Mr. Conried, we shall not be here tonight. Our eight-hour day expires at five o'clock."[245]

*****

• Follow your bliss. Ron Shelton, a minor-league baseball player, was fascinated by director Sam Peckinpah's *The Wild Bunch* when it first appeared in movie theaters. He saw it at least once every day for two weeks, risking his job because he began to arrive late at the ballpark. After seeing the movie, he decided to become a film director. Now, he is known as the director of *Bull Durham* and *White Men Can't Jump*.[246]

• Phil Baker was both a comedian and an accordion player. Even though he was not a very good accordion player, a manufacturer of accordions once asked him to endorse its products. Mr. Baker asked, "How come you selected me? There are a lot of better accordion players." The answer came back, "I know, but you're the only one who's working steadily."[247]

• Like many writers, Quentin Tarantino, famous for his movies *Reservoir Dogs*, *Pulp Fiction*, and *Jackie Brown*, worked at many odd jobs before becoming famous. He once worked on a workout video starring Dolph Lundgren. (Mr. Tarantino's job was cleaning doggy doodoo off the parking lot so Mr. Lundgren wouldn't get his outfit dirty.)[248]

• A teacher let her 1st-grade students know that after returning from work, she liked to sew. One of her students asked, "Where do you work?" In another classroom, a student asked her teacher the same question. Of course, the teacher said, "Here. This is my job — teaching." The student was shocked: "You mean you get *paid* for this?"[249]

• As a salesman, Myron Cohen told a lot of funny stories to his customers. One day, his boss talked to him and said, "Myron, you're a wonderful, funny guy and you should be paid for telling those stories of yours — but not by me!" So Mr. Cohen became a professional comedian.[250]

Appendix A: Bibliography

Aaseng, Nathan. *American Dinosaur Hunters*. Springfield, NJ: Enslow Publications, Inc., 1996.

Adler, Bill. *Jewish Wit and Wisdom*. New York: Dell Publishing Co., Inc, 1969.

Adler, Bill, and Bruce Cassiday. *The World of Jay Leno: His Humor and His Life*. New York: Carol Publishing Group, 1992.

Allen, Steve. *More Funny People*. New York: Stein and Day, Publishers, 1982.

Anderson, Margaret J. *Charles Darwin: Naturalist*. Hillside, NJ: Enslow Publications, Inc. 1994.

Anderson, Margaret J., and Karen F. Stevenson. *Scientists of the Ancient World*. Berkeley Heights, NJ: Enslow Publications, Inc., 1999.

Arden, Eve. *Three Phases of Eve: An Autobiography*. New York: St. Martin's Press, 1985.

Ashley, Merrill. *Dancing for Balanchine*. New York: E.P. Dutton, Inc., 1984.

Banks, Morwenna, and Amanda Swift. *The Joke's on Us: Women in Comedy from Music Hall to the Present Day*. London: Pandora Press, 1987.

Benchley, Nathaniel. *Robert Benchley*. New York: McGraw-Hill Book Company, Inc., 1955.

Berger, Phil. *The Last Laugh: The World of the Stand-Up Comics*. New York: William Morris and Co., Inc., 1975.

Bernard, André. *Now All We Need is a Title: Famous Book Titles and How They Got That Way*. New York: W.W. Norton & Company, 1995.

Bing, Sir Rudolf. *5000 Nights at the Opera*. Garden City, NY: Doubleday and Company, Inc., 1972.

Borns, Betsy. *Comic Lives: Inside the World of American Stand-Up Comedy*. New York: Simon and Schuster, Inc., 1987.

Boxer, Tim. *The Jewish Celebrity Hall of Fame*. New York: Shapolsky Publishers, 1987.

Brandreth, Gyles. *Great Theatrical Disasters*. New York: St. Martin's Press, 1982.

Briggs, Joe Bob. *Profoundly Disturbing: Shocking Movies That Changed History!* New York: Universe Books, 2003.

Brown, Michèle and Ann O'Connor. *Hammer and Tongues: A Dictionary of Women's Wit and Humour*. London: J.M. Dent and Sons, Ltd., 1986.

Bryan III, J. *Merry Gentlemen (and One Lady)*. New York: Atheneum, 1985.

Bryson, Bill. *The Mother Tongue: English & How It Got That Way*. New York: William Morrow and Company, Inc., 1990.

Burke, John. *Rogue's Progress: The Fabulous Adventures of Wilson Mizner*. New York: G.P. Putnam's Sons, 1975.

Camp, Carole Ann. *American Astronomers*. Springfield, NJ: Enslow Publications, Inc., 1996.

Cantor, Eddie. *As I Remember Them*. New York: Duell, Sloan and Pearce, 1963. (Mr. Cantor's collaborator for most of these pieces was Vivian M. Bowes, to whom he gives credit on the acknowledgements page.)

Carpenter, Angelica Shirley, and Jean Shirley. *Frances Hodgson Burnett: Beyond the Secret Garden*. Minneapolis, MN: Lerner Publications Company, 1990.

Carpenter, Angelica Shirley, and Jean Shirley. *L. Frank Baum: Royal Historian of Oz*. Minneapolis, MN: Lerner Publications Company, 1992.

Carter, Judy. *The Homo Handbook*. New York: Fireside Books, 1996.

Carter, Judy. *Stand-Up Comedy: The Book*. New York: Dell Publishing, 1989.

Chapman, Graham. *Graham Crackers*. Compiled by Jim Yoakum. Franklin Lakes, NJ: Career Press, Inc., 1997.

Cho, Margaret. *I'm the One That I Want*. New York: Ballantine Books, 2001.

Clemens, Cyril. *Chesterton As Seen by His Contemporaries*. New York: Haskell House Publishers, Ltd., 1969.

Clemens, Cyril, editor. *Mark Twain Anecdotes*. Webster Groves, MO: Mark Twain Society, 1929.

Clercq, Tanaquil Le. *The Ballet Cook Book*. New York: Stein and Day, Publishers, 1966.

Clinton, Kate. *Don't Get Me Started*. New York: Ballantine Books, 1998.

Cohen, Myron. *Laughing Out Loud*. New York: The Citadel Press, 1958.

Cole, Michael D. *John Glenn: Astronaut and Senator*. Hillside, NJ: Enslow Publications, Inc., 1993.

Crow, Bill. *Jazz Anecdotes*. New York: Oxford University Press, 1990.

Dean, Greg. *Step by Step to Stand-Up Comedy*. Portsmouth, NH: Heinemann, 2000.

Dickinson, Joan D. *Bill Gates: Billionaire Computer Genius*. Springfield, NJ: Enslow Publications, Inc., 1997.

Drennan, Robert E., editor. *The Algonquin Wits*. New York: The Citadel Press, 1968.

Eichenbaum, Rose. *Masters of Movement: Portraits of America's Great Choreographers*. Washington DC: Smithsonian Books, 2004.

Epstein, Lawrence J. *George Burns: An American Life*. Jefferson, NC, and London: McFarland & Company, Inc., Publishers, 2011.

Finck, Henry T. *My Adventures in the Golden Age of Music*. New York and London: Funk & Wagnalls Company, 1926.

Fine, Edith Hope. *Barbara McClintock: Nobel Prize Geneticist.* Springfield, NJ: Enslow Publications, Inc., 1998.

Ford, Corey. *The Time of Laughter.* Boston, MA: Little, Brown and Company, 1967.

Foxx, Redd, and Norma Miller. *The Redd Foxx Encyclopedia of Black Humor.* Pasadena, CA: Ward Ritchie Press, 1977.

Franklin, Joe. *Joe Franklin's Encyclopedia of Comedians.* Secaucus, NJ: The Citadel Press, 1979.

Freberg, Stan. *It Only Hurts When I Laugh.* New York: Times Books, 1988.

Funny Gay Males (a comedy troupe consisting of Jaffe Cohen, Danny McWilliams, and Bob Smith). *Growing Up Gay.* New York: Hyperion, 1995.

Gallo, Hank. *Comedy Explosion: A New Generation.* Photographs by Ed Edahl. New York: Thunder's Mouth Press, 1991.

Garfunkle, Trudy. *On Wings of Joy: The Story of Ballet from the 16th Century to Today.* Boston, MA: Little, Brown and Company, 1994.

Garner, Joe. *Now Showing: Unforgettable Moments from the Movies.* Kansas City, MO: Andrews McMeel Publishing, 2003.

Gitenstein, Judy. *Alvin Ailey.* New York: The Rosen Publishing Group, Inc., 2006.

Gold, Rebecca. *Steve Wozniak: A Wizard Called Woz.* Minneapolis, MN: Lerner Publications Company, 1994.

Goodman, Jack, and Albert Rice. *I Wish I'd Said That!* New York: Simon and Schuster, 1935.

Gottlieb, Robert. *George Balanchine: The Ballet Maker.* New York: HarperCollins Publishers, Inc., 2004.

Grenfell, Joyce. *Joyce Grenfell Requests the Pleasure.* London: Macdonald Futura Publishers Ltd., 1976.

Guttmacher, Peter. *Legendary Comedies.* New York: MetroBooks, 1996.

Halliwell, Leslie. *The Filmgoer's Book of Quotes.* New Rochelle, NY: Arlington House Publishers, 1973.

Harmon, Jim. *The Great Radio Comedians.* Garden City, NY: Doubleday and Company, Inc., 1970.

Hecht, Ben. *Charlie: The Improbable Life and Times of Charles MacArthur.* New York: Harper & Brothers, Publishers, 1957.

Henry, Lewis C. *Humorous Anecdotes About Famous People.* Garden City, NY: Halcyon House, 1948.

Hill, Christine M. *Ten Terrific Authors for Teens.* Berkeley Heights, NJ: Enslow Publications, Inc., 2000.

Hodges, Diane. *Laugh Lines for Educators*. Thousand Oaks, California: Corwin Press, 2006.

Hodgson, Moira. *Quintet: Five American Dance Companies*. Photographs by Thomas Victor. New York: William Morrow and Company, Inc., 1976.

Holland, Merlin. *The Wilde Album*. New York: Henry Holt and Company, 1997.

Holloway, Stanley. *Wiv a Little Bit O' Luck*. As told to Dick Richards. New York: Stein and Day, Publishers, 1967.

Horowitz, Susan. *Queens of Comedy*. Australia: Gordon and Breach Publishers, 1997.

Johnson, Rebecca L. *Science on the Ice: An Antarctic Journal*. Minneapolis, MN: Lerner Publications Company, 1995.

Johnson, Russell, and Steve Cox. *Here on Gilligan's Isle*. New York: HarperCollins Publishers, Inc., 1993.

Josephson, Judith Pinkerton. *Nikki Giovanni: Poet of the People*. Berkeley Heights, NJ: Enslow Publications, Inc., 2000.

Kallen, Stuart A. *Great Male Comedians*. San Diego, CA: Lucent Books, 2001.

Kanner, Bernice. *The 100 Best TV Commercials ... and Why They Worked*. New York: Times Books, 1999.

Kent, Allegra. *Once a Dancer ...*. New York: St. Martin's Press, 1997.

Kramer, Barbara. *Amy Tan: Author of* The Joy Luck Club. Springfield, NJ: Enslow Publications, Inc., 1996.

Krohn, Katherine E. *Marilyn Monroe: Norma Jeane's Dream*. Minneapolis, MN: Lerner Publications Company, 1997.

Laffey, Bruce. *Beatrice Lillie: The Funniest Woman in the World*. New York: Wynwood Press, 1989.

Leno, Jay. *Leading With My Chin*. With Bill Zehme. New York: HarperCollins Publishers, Inc., 1996.

Leonard, Sheldon. *And the Show Goes On: Broadway and Hollywood Adventures*. New York: Limelight, 1994.

Northrup, Mary. *American Computer Pioneers*. Springfield, NJ: Enslow Publications, Inc., 1998.

Pearson, Hesketh. *Lives of the Wits*. New York: Harper & Row, Publishers, 1962.

Pelta, Kathy. *Bridging the Golden Gate*. Minneapolis, MN: Lerner Publications Company, 1987.

Peterson, T.F. *Nightwork: A History of Hacks and Pranks at MIT*. Cambridge, Massachusetts: MIT Press, 2011.

Pratt, Paula Bryant. *Martha Graham*. San Diego, CA: Lucent Books, 1995.

Primack, Ben, adapter and editor. *The Ben Hecht Show: Impolitic Observations from the Freest Thinker of 1950s Television*. Jefferson, NC: McFarland & Company, Inc., Publishers, 1993.

Richards, Dick, compiler. *The Wit of Noël Coward*. London: Leslie Frewin, 1968.

Richards, Dick, compiler. *The Wit of Peter Ustinov*. London: Leslie Frewin Publishers, Limited, 1969.

Rutkowska, Wanda. *Famous People in Anecdotes*. Warszawa: Wydawnictwa Szkolne i Pedagogiczne, 1977.

Schafer, Kermit. *The Bedside Book of Celebrity Bloopers*. New York: Crown Publishers, Inc., 1984.

Schafer, Kermit. *Best of Bloopers*. New York: Avenel Books, 1973.

Scherer, Barrymore Laurence. *Bravo! A Guide to Opera for the Perplexed*. New York: Dutton, 1996.

Shawn, Ted. *One Thousand and One Night Stands*. With Gray Poole. New York: Da Capo Press, Inc., 1979.

Sheafer, Silvia Anne. *Aretha Franklin: Motown Superstar*. Springfield, NJ: Enslow Publications, Inc., 1996.

Shindler, Phyllis, collector. *Raise Your Glasses*. London: Judy Piatkus, Limited, 1988.

Slezak, Leo. *Song of Motley*. New York: Arno Press, 1977.

Slezak, Walter. *What Time's the Next Swan?* Garden City, NY: Doubleday and Co., Inc., 1962.

Smith, H. Allen. *Buskin' With H. Allen Smith*. New York: Trident Press, 1968.

Smith, H. Allen. *The Compleat Practical Joker*. Garden City, NY: Doubleday and Company, Inc., 1953.

Sorel, Nancy Caldwell, and Edward Sorel. *First Encounters: A Book of Memorable Meetings*. New York: Alfred A. Knopf, 1994.

Story, Rosalyn M. *And So I Sing: African-American Divas of Opera and Concert*. New York: Warner Books, 1990.

Sykes, Adam, and Iain Sproat, compilers. *The Wit of Westminster*. London: Leslie Frewin, Limited, 1967.

Szilard, Paul. *Under My Wings: My Life as an Impresario*. New York: Limelight Editions, 2002.

Tallchief, Maria. *Maria Tallchief: America's Prima Ballerina*. With Larry Kaplan. New York: Henry Holt and Company, 1997.

Taylor, Glenhall. *Before Television: The Radio Years*. New York: A.S. Barnes and Company, 1979.

Teachout, Terry. *All in the Dances: A Brief Life of George Balanchine*. New York: Harcourt, Inc., 2004.

Terry, Walter. *Frontiers of Dance: The Life of Martha Graham*. New York: Thomas Y. Crowell Company, 1975.

Terry, Walter. *Star Performance: The Story of the World's Great Ballerinas*. Garden City, New York: Doubleday & Co., Inc., 1954.

Tingum, Janice. *E.B. White: The Elements of a Writer*. Minneapolis, MN: Lerner Publications Company, 1995.

Tobias, Andrew. *The Best Little Boy in the World Grows Up*. New York: Random House, 1998.

Towse, John Rankin. *Sixty Years of the Theater: An Old Critic's Memories*. New York and London: Funk & Wagnalls Company, 1916.

Tracy, Robert, and Sharon DeLano. *Balanchine's Ballerinas: Conversations with the Muses*. New York: Linden Press/Simon and Schuster, 1983.

Tully, Jim. *A Dozen and One*. Hollywood, CA: Murray & Gee, Inc., Publishers, 1943.

Van Dyke, Dick. *Those Funny Kids!* Garden City, NY: Doubleday and Company, Inc., 1975.

Vaswani, J.P. *The Good You Do Returns: A Book of Wisdom Stories*. Liguori, Missouri: Triumph Books, 1995.

Vickers, Hugh. *Even Greater Operatic Disasters*. New York: St. Martin's Press, 1982.

Villella, Edward. *Prodigal Son: Dancing for Balanchine in a World of Pain and Magic*. With Larry Kaplan. New York: Simon and Schuster, 1992.

Voskressenski, Alexei D., compiler and editor. *Cranks, Knaves, and Jokers of the Celestial*. Translated from the Chinese by Alexei Voskressenski and Vladimir Larin. Commack, NY: Nova Science Publishers, Inc., 1997.

Wadsworth, Ginger. *Laura Ingalls Wilder: Storyteller of the Prairie*. Minneapolis, MN: Lerner Publications Company, 1997.

Wagner, Alan. *Prima Donnas and Other Wild Beasts*. Larchmont, NY: Argonaut Books, 1961.

Warren, Roz, editor. *Dyke Strippers: Lesbian Cartoonists A to Z*. Pittsburgh, PA: Cleis Press, Inc., 1995.

Wasserman, Harriet. *Handsome Is: Adventures with Saul Bellow*. New York: Fromm International Publishing Company, 1997.

Waters, John. *Shock Value*. New York: Dell Publishing Company, Inc., 1981.

Watson, Richard. *The Philosopher's Diet: How to Lose Weight and Change the World*. Boston, MA: The Atlantic Monthly Press, 1985.

Weissman, Ginny, and Coyne Steven Sanders. *The Dick Van Dyke Show*. New York: St. Martin's Press, 1993.

Williams, Kenneth. *Acid Drops*. London: J. M. Dent & Sons, Ltd., 1980.

Woog, Adam. *Magicians and Illusionists*. San Diego, CA: Lucent Books, 2000.

Yount, Lisa. *Antoine Lavoisier: Founder of Modern Chemistry*. Springfield, NJ: Enslow Publications, Inc., 1997.

Zall, Paul M. *The Wit and Wisdom of the Founding Fathers*. Hopewell, NJ: The Ecco Press, 1996.

Zolotow, Maurice. *No People Like Show People*. New York: Random House, 1951.

Appendix B: About the Author

It was a dark and stormy night. Suddenly a cry rang out, and on a hot summer night in 1954, Josephine, wife of Carl Bruce, gave birth to a boy — me. Unfortunately, this young married couple allowed Reuben Saturday, Josephine's brother, to name their first-born. Reuben, aka "The Joker," decided that Bruce was a nice name, so he decided to name me Bruce Bruce. I have gone by my middle name — David — ever since.

Being named Bruce David Bruce hasn't been all bad. Bank tellers remember me very quickly, so I don't often have to show an ID. It can be fun in charades, also. When I was a counselor as a teenager at Camp Echoing Hills in Warsaw, Ohio, a fellow counselor gave the signs for "sounds like" and "two words," then she pointed to a bruise on her leg twice. Bruise Bruise? Oh yeah, Bruce Bruce is the answer!

Uncle Reuben, by the way, gave me a haircut when I was in kindergarten. He cut my hair short and shaved a small bald spot on the back of my head. My mother wouldn't let me go to school until the bald spot grew out again.

Of all my brothers and sisters (six in all), I am the only transplant to Athens, Ohio. I was born in Newark, Ohio, and have lived all around Southeastern Ohio. However, I moved to Athens to go to Ohio University and have never left.

At Ohio U, I never could make up my mind whether to major in English or Philosophy, so I got a bachelor's degree with a double major in both areas, then I added a Master of Arts degree in English and a Master of Arts degree in Philosophy. Yes, I have my MAMA degree.

Currently, and for a long time to come (I eat fruits and veggies), I am spending my retirement writing books such as *Nadia Comaneci: Perfect 10*, *The Funniest People in Comedy*, *Homer's* Iliad: *A Retelling in Prose*, and *William Shakespeare's* Hamlet: *A Retelling in Prose*.

If all goes well, I will publish one or two books a year for the rest of my life. (On the other hand, a good way to make God laugh is to tell Her your plans.)

By the way, my sister Brenda Kennedy writes romances such as *A New Beginning* and *Shattered Dreams*.

Appendix C: Some Books by David Bruce

Anecdote Collections

250 Anecdotes About Opera

250 Anecdotes About Religion

250 Anecdotes About Religion: Volume 2

250 Music Anecdotes

Be a Work of Art: 250 Anecdotes and Stories

The Coolest People in Art: 250 Anecdotes

The Coolest People in the Arts: 250 Anecdotes

The Coolest People in Books: 250 Anecdotes

The Coolest People in Comedy: 250 Anecdotes

Create, Then Take a Break: 250 Anecdotes

Don't Fear the Reaper: 250 Anecdotes

The Funniest People in Art: 250 Anecdotes

The Funniest People in Books: 250 Anecdotes

The Funniest People in Books, Volume 2: 250 Anecdotes

The Funniest People in Books, Volume 3: 250 Anecdotes

The Funniest People in Comedy: 250 Anecdotes

The Funniest People in Dance: 250 Anecdotes

The Funniest People in Families: 250 Anecdotes

The Funniest People in Families, Volume 2: 250 Anecdotes

The Funniest People in Families, Volume 3: 250 Anecdotes

The Funniest People in Families, Volume 4: 250 Anecdotes

The Funniest People in Families, Volume 5: 250 Anecdotes

The Funniest People in Families, Volume 6: 250 Anecdotes

The Funniest People in Movies: 250 Anecdotes

The Funniest People in Music: 250 Anecdotes

The Funniest People in Music, Volume 2: 250 Anecdotes

The Funniest People in Music, Volume 3: 250 Anecdotes

The Funniest People in Neighborhoods: 250 Anecdotes

The Funniest People in Relationships: 250 Anecdotes

The Funniest People in Sports: 250 Anecdotes

The Funniest People in Sports, Volume 2: 250 Anecdotes

The Funniest People in Television and Radio: 250 Anecdotes

The Funniest People in Theater: 250 Anecdotes

The Funniest People Who Live Life: 250 Anecdotes

The Funniest People Who Live Life, Volume 2: 250 Anecdotes

The Kindest People Who Do Good Deeds, Volume 1: 250 Anecdotes

The Kindest People Who Do Good Deeds, Volume 2: 250 Anecdotes

Maximum Cool: 250 Anecdotes

The Most Interesting People in Movies: 250 Anecdotes

The Most Interesting People in Politics and History: 250 Anecdotes

The Most Interesting People in Politics and History, Volume 2: 250 Anecdotes

The Most Interesting People in Politics and History, Volume 3: 250 Anecdotes

The Most Interesting People in Religion: 250 Anecdotes

The Most Interesting People in Sports: 250 Anecdotes

The Most Interesting People Who Live Life: 250 Anecdotes

The Most Interesting People Who Live Life, Volume 2: 250 Anecdotes

Reality is Fabulous: 250 Anecdotes and Stories

Resist Psychic Death: 250 Anecdotes

Seize the Day: 250 Anecdotes and Stories

[1] Source: John Rankin Towse, *Sixty Years of the Theater: An Old Critic's Memories*, pp. 194-195.

[2] Source: Sheldon Leonard, *And the Show Goes On*, pp. 29-30.

[3] Source: Stanley Holloway, *Wiv a Little Bit O' Luck*, pp. 222-223.

[4] Source: John Waters, *Shock Value*, p. 128.

[5] Source: "Coca-Cola vending machine delivers a Coke and a smile." Ogilvy and Mather. 5 April 2012 <http://www.ogilvy.com/News/Press-Releases/April-2012-Coca-Cola-vending-machine-delivers-a-Coke-and-a-smile.aspx>.

[6] Source: Adam Woog, *Magicians and Illusionists*, p. 40.

[7] Source: Stan Freberg, *It Only Hurts When I Laugh*, pp. 78, 183.

[8] Source: Andrew Tobias, *The Best Little Boy in the World Grows Up*, pp. 117, 169.

[9] Source: Dick Richards, compiler, *The Wit of Noël Coward*, pp. 51, 99.

[10] Source: John Waters, *Shock Value*, p. 83.

[11] Source: T.F. Peterson, *Nightwork: A History of Hacks and Pranks at MIT*, pp. 102-103, 106.

[12] Source: Rob Stevens, "Angel with a mobile phone." Rob's Webstek. 16 April 2011 <http://www.robswebstek.com/2011/04/angel-with-mobile-phone.html>.

[13] Source: Lewis C. Henry, *Humorous Anecdotes About Famous People*, pp. 20-21.

[14] Source: Betsy Borns, *Comic Lives*, pp. 132-133.

[15] Source: Walter Terry, *Frontiers of Dance: The Life of Martha Graham*, p. 61.

[16] Source: Russell Johnson and Steve Cox, *Here on Gilligan's Isle*, pp. 17-18.

[17] Source: Trudy Garfunkle, *On Wings of Joy*, p. 150.

[18] Source: Rose Eichenbaum, *Masters of Movement: Portraits of America's Great Choreographers*, pp. 112-115.

[19] Source: Tanaquil Le Clercq, *The Ballet Cook Book*, pp. 147-148.

[20] Source: Ginger Wadsworth, *Laura Ingalls Wilder: Storyteller of the Prairie*, pp. 30, 76.

[21] Source: Janice Tingum, *E.B. White: The Elements of a Writer*, pp. 11-12, 50, 103.

[22] Source: André Bernard, *Now All We Need is a Title*, p. 112.

[23] Source: Bernice Kanner, *The 100 Best TV Commercials*, pp. 206-207.

[24] Source: Harriet Wasserman, *Handsome Is: Adventures with Saul Bellow*, p. 17.

[25] Source: Steve Allen, *More Funny People*, book jacket.

[26] Source: Corey Ford, *The Time of Laughter*, p. 194.

[27] Source: Kermit Schafer, *Best of Bloopers*, pp. 10, 22, 106.

[28] Source: Kermit Schafer, *The Bedside Book of Celebrity Bloopers*, p. 71.

[29] Source: Margaret J. Anderson and Karen F. Stevenson, *Scientists of the Ancient World*, pp. 47-48.

[30] Source: Lewis C. Henry, *Humorous Anecdotes About Famous People*, p. 34.

[31] Source: Kathy Pelta, *Bridging the Golden Gate*, pp. 79-81.

[32] Source: T.F. Peterson, *Nightwork: A History of Hacks and Pranks at MIT*, pp. 142-145.

[33] Source: Paul Harris and Lucy Laing, "Closer than ever... The million-to-one black and white twins Kian and Remee turn seven." *Daily Mail* (UK). 30 March 2012 <http://www.dailymail.co.uk/news/article-2123050/Look-The-black-white-twins-turn-seven.html?ICO=most_read_module>.

[34] Source: Ginger Wadsworth, *Laura Ingalls Wilder: Storyteller of the Prairie*, pp. 30, 48-49, 108.

[35] Source: Janice Tingum, *E.B. White: The Elements of a Writer*, pp. 77, 108, 115.

[36] Source: Angelica Shirley Carpenter and Jean Shirley, *Frances Hodgson Burnett: Beyond the Secret Garden*, pp. 40, 64.

[37] Source: J.P. Vaswani, *The Good You Do Returns: A Book of Wisdom Stories*, p. 105.

[38] Source: Diane Hodges, *Laugh Lines for Educators*, pp. 70-71.

[39] Source: Margaret J. Anderson, *Charles Darwin: Naturalist*, pp. 7, 73, 75.

[40] Source: Walter Terry, *Frontiers of Dance: The Life of Martha Graham*, p. 32.

[41] Source: Christine M. Hill, *Ten Terrific Authors for Teens*, p. 61.

[42] Source: J. Bryan III, *Merry Gentlemen (and One Lady)*, p. 94.

[43] Source: Carole Ann Camp, *American Astronomers*, pp. 69-70.

[44] Source: Rose Eichenbaum, *Masters of Movement: Portraits of America's Great Choreographers*, p. 90.

[45] Source: Moira Hodgson, *Quintet: Five American Dance Companies*, p. 13.

[46] Source: Angelica Shirley Carpenter and Jean Shirley, *L. Frank Baum: Royal Historian of Oz*, pp. 39, 52.

[47] Source: Stuart A. Kallen, *Great Male Comedians*, pp. 68, 70.

[48] Source: Ginny Weissman and Coyne Steven Sanders, *The Dick Van Dyke Show*, p. 95.

[49] Source: Bruce Laffey, *Beatrice Lillie*, pp. 234-235.

[50] Source: Morwenna Banks and Amanda Swift, *The Joke's on Us*, p. 87.

[51] Source: Wanda Rutkowska, *Famous People in Anecdotes*, p. 57.

[52] Source: Jim Harmon, *The Great Radio Comedians*, pp. 174-175, 180.

[53] Source: Myron Cohen, *Laughing Out Loud*, pp. 159-160, 168.

[54] Source: Susan Horowitz, *Queens of Comedy*, p. 45.

[55] Source: Morwenna Banks and Amanda Swift, *The Joke's on Us*, p. 15.

[56] Source: Bill Adler and Bruce Cassiday, *The World of Jay Leno: His Humor and His Life*, pp. 23-24.

[57] Source: Walter Terry, *Star Performance*, p. 174.

[58] Source: Graham Chapman, *Graham Crackers*, pp. 13, 57.

[59] Source: Jay Leno, *Leading With My Chin*, pp. 204-205.

[60] Source: Phil Berger, *The Last Laugh*, p. 34.

[61] Source: Eddie Cantor, *As I Remember Them*, p. 100.

[62] Source: Susan Horowitz, *Queens of Comedy*, p. 153.

[63] Source: Margaret Cho, *I'm the One That I Want*, p. 28.

[64] Source: Phil Berger, *The Last Laugh*, p. 72.

[65] Source: Hank Gallo, *Comedy Explosion: A New Generation*, p. 83.

[66] Source: Judy Carter, *Stand-Up Comedy: The Book*, p. 154.

[67] Source: Henry T. Finck, *My Adventures in the Golden Age of Music*, pp. 266, 327, 337.

[68] Source: Rosalyn M. Story, *And So I Sing: African-American Divas of Opera and Concert*, pp. 111-112.

[69] Source: Paul Szilard, *Under My Wings*, p. 12.

[70] Source: Edward Villella, *Prodigal Son: Dancing for Balanchine in a World of Pain and Magic*, p. 147.

[71] Source: Ted Shawn, *One Thousand and One Night Stands*, pp. 238-239.

[72] Source: Tanaquil Le Clercq, *The Ballet Cook Book*, p. 229.

[73] Source: Redd Foxx and Norma Miller, *The Redd Foxx Encyclopedia of Black Humor*, p. 228.

[74] Source: Paul M. Zall, *The Wit and Wisdom of the Founding Fathers*, pp. 10, 13, 39-40.

[75] Source: "Obituary or Memoriam: Michael 'Flathead' Blanchard." *Denver Post* (Colorado). 12 April 2012 <http://www.legacy.com/obituaries/denverpost/obituary.aspx?page=lifestory&pid=156944598>.

[76] Source: Graham Chapman, *Graham Crackers*, book jacket, pp. 7, 162.

[77] Source: Paul M. Zall, *The Wit and Wisdom of the Founding Fathers*, pp. 125, 137.

[78] Source: Rebecca Gold, *Steve Wozniak: A Wizard Called Woz*, pp. 22-23, 29.

[79] Source: Stuart A. Kallen, *Great Male Comedians*, pp. 42-43, 50.

[80] Source: Alexei D. Voskressenski, compiler and editor, *Cranks, Knaves, and Jokers of the Celestial*, p. 100.

[81] Source: Kate Clinton, *Don't Get Me Started*, pp. 135-136.

[82] Source: Bill Adler and Bruce Cassiday, *The World of Jay Leno: His Humor and His Life*, pp. 8, 21.

[83] Source: Merrill Ashley, *Dancing for Balanchine*, p. 196.

[84] Source: Merrill Ashley, *Dancing for Balanchine*, pp. 233-234.

[85] Source: Dick Van Dyke, *Those Funny Kids!*, p. 13.

[86] Source: Maria Tallchief, *Maria Tallchief: America's Prima Ballerina*, pp. 169.

[87] Source: Terry Teachout, *All in the Dances: A Brief Life of George Balanchine*, p. 60.

[88] Source: Barrymore Laurence Scherer, *Bravo! A Guide to Opera for the Perplexed*, p. 83, 229.

[89] Source: Moira Hodgson, *Quintet: Five American Dance Companies*, pp. 120-121.

[90] Source: Phyllis Shindler, collector, *Raise Your Glasses*, p. 20.

[91] Source: Silvia Anne Sheafer, *Aretha Franklin: Motown Superstar*, p. 20.

[92] Source: Bob Hope, *The Road to Hollywood*, pp. 10, 32.

[93] Source: Jim Tully, *A Dozen and One*, p. 16.

[94] Source: Jay Leno, *Leading With My Chin*, p. 211.

[95] Source: Lawrence J. Epstein, *George Burns: An American Life*, pp. 74-75.

[96] Source: Maurice Zolotow, *No People Like Show People*, p. 233.

[97] Source: Richard Watson, *The Philosopher's Diet*, p. 53.

[98] Source: Jack Goodman and Albert Rice, *I Wish I'd Said That!*, p. 80.

[99] Source: Walter Terry, *Star Performance*, pp. 58-59, 64.

[100] Source: Robert Gottlieb, *George Balanchine: The Ballet Maker*, p. 75.

[101] Source: Lawrence J. Epstein, *George Burns: An American Life*, p. 104.

[102] Source: Nancy Caldwell Sorel and Edward Sorel, *First Encounters*, p. 99.

[103] Source: Russell Johnson and Steve Cox, *Here on Gilligan's Isle*, p. 105.

[104] Source: J.P. Vaswani, *The Good You Do Returns: A Book of Wisdom Stories*, pp. 15-16.

[105] Source: Robert E. Drennan, ed., *The Algonquin Wits*, pp. 30-31.

[106] Source: Judy Carter, *The Homo Handbook*, p. 20, 98, 187.

[107] Source: Terry Teachout, *All in the Dances: A Brief Life of George Balanchine*, pp. 34-35.

[108] Source: Funny Gay Males, *Growing Up Gay*, p. 139.

[109] Source: Kate Clinton, *Don't Get Me Started*, p. 25.

[110] Source: Andrew Tobias, "Man With A Clear Conscience." 9 April 2012 <http://andrewtobias.com/column/man-with-a-clear-conscience/>.

[111] Source: Judy Gitenstein, *Alvin Ailey*, pp. 9-10.

[112] Source: "$10,000 LEMONADE STAND." KTRH. 18 April 2012 <http://www.mega949.com/cc-common/news/sections/newsarticle.html?feed=104673&article=10058935>.

[113] Source: Nathaniel Benchley, *Robert Benchley*, pp. 13-14.

[114] Source: Bruce Laffey, *Beatrice Lillie*, pp. 93, 167.

[115] Source: Cyril Clemens, *Chesterton As Seen by His Contemporaries*, p. 23.

[116] Source: Sir Rudolf Bing, *5000 Nights at the Opera*, pp. 271-272.

[117] Source: Michèle Brown and Ann O'Connor, *Hammer and Tongues*, p. 64.

[118] Source: Phyllis Shindler, collector, *Raise Your Glasses*, p. 75.

[119] Source: Joyce Grenfell, *Joyce Grenfell Requests the Pleasure*, p. 213, 214, 221.

[120] Source: Cyril Clemens, editor, *Mark Twain Anecdotes*, pp. 18-19.

[121] Source: Robert E. Drennan, ed., *The Algonquin Wits*, p. 142.

[122] Source: H. Allen Smith, *Buskin' With H. Allen Smith*, p. 174.

[123] Source: Bill Bryson, *The Mother Tongue*, p. 146.

[124] Source: Norman Maclean, "The End of the World of Books." Letters of Note. 16 April 2012 <http://www.lettersofnote.com/2012/04/end-of-world-of-books.html>.

[125] Source: Judith Pinkerton Josephson, *Nikki Giovanni: Poet of the People*, pp. 20, 26.

[126] Source: Revstephmc, "Love — The Long and Short of It!" Helpothers.org. 27 March 2012 <http://www.helpothers.org/story.php?sid=30388>.

[127] Source: H. Allen Smith, *The Compleat Practical Joker*, p. 280.

[128] Source: J. Bryan III, *Merry Gentlemen (and One Lady)*, p. 210.

[129] Source: Edith Hope Fine, *Barbara McClintock: Nobel Prize Geneticist*, p. 11.

[130] Source: Richard Watson, *The Philosopher's Diet*, pp. 105-106.

[131] Source: Ana Samways, "Rescue Dwarfs All Others." *New Zealand Herald*. 12 April 2012 <http://www.nzherald.co.nz/opinion/news/article.cfm?c_id=466&objectid=10798150>.

[132] Source: Judy Carter, *Stand-Up Comedy: The Book*, pp. 109, 117.

[133] Source: Cyril Clemens, *Chesterton As Seen by His Contemporaries*, pp. 31-32, 167.

[134] Source: Greg Dean, *Step by Step to Stand-Up Comedy*, p. 163.

[135] Source: Hugh Vickers, *Even Greater Operatic Disasters*, p. 78.

[136] Source: Glenhall Taylor, *Before Television*, p. 94,

[137] Source: Leo Slezak, *Song of Motley*, pp. 85-86.

[138] Source: Hugh Vickers, *Even Greater Operatic Disasters*, p. 54.

[139] Source: Allegra Kent, *Once a Dancer ...*, p. 46.

[140] Source: Joan D. Dickinson, *Bill Gates: Billionaire Computer Genius*, pp. 69, 74.

[141] Source: Peter Guttmacher, *Legendary Comedies*, pp. 18, 20.

[142] Source: Walter Slezak, *What Time's the Next Swan?*, pp. 34-35.

[143] Source: Sheldon Leonard, *And the Show Goes On*, pp. 43-44.

[144] Source: Cyril Clemens, editor, *Mark Twain Anecdotes*, p. 14.

[145] Source: Paul Szilard, *Under My Wings*, p. 31.

[146] Source: Hank Gallo, *Comedy Explosion: A New Generation*, p. 30.

[147] Source: Jim Harmon, *The Great Radio Comedians*, p. 158.

[148] Source: Steve Allen, *More Funny People*, p. 275.

[149] Source: Barbara Kramer, *Amy Tan: Author of* The Joy Luck Club, pp. 10, 67.

[150] Source: "What's the Greatest Gift Your Mother Ever Gave You?" *Real Simple*. Posted on Dailygood,org. <http://www.dailygood.org/more.php?n=4967>. Accessed on 21 April 2012.

[151] Source: Harriet Wasserman, *Handsome Is: Adventures with Saul Bellow*, pp. 141-142.

[152] Source: Roz Warren, editor, *Dyke Strippers: Lesbian Cartoonists A to Z*, p. 203.

[153] Source: Robert Tracy and Sharon DeLano, *Balanchine's Ballerinas: Conversations with the Muses*, p. 53.

[154] Source: Silvia Anne Sheafer, *Aretha Franklin: Motown Superstar*, pp. 14, 69-70, 95.

[155] Source: Maurice Zolotow, *No People Like Show People*, pp. 136, 142, 149.

[156] Source: Alan Wagner, *Prima Donnas and Other Wild Beasts*, p. 234.

[157] Source: Bill Adler, *Jewish Wit and Wisdom*, pp. 20-21.

[158] Source: Joe Franklin, *Joe Franklin's Encyclopedia of Comedians*, p. 317.

[159] Source: Stan Freberg, *It Only Hurts When I Laugh*, pp. 7-8.

[160] Source: Allegra Kent, *Once a Dancer ...*, pp. 5, 7, 23-24.

[161] Source: André Bernard, *Now All We Need is a Title*, p. 15.

[162] Source: J. Edward Evans, *Charles Darwin: Revolutionary Biologist*, pp. 37-38.

[163] Source: Bill Crow, *Jazz Anecdotes*, p. vi.

[164] Source: Hesketh Pearson, *Lives of the Wits*, pp. 243-244.

[165] Source: Rebecca Gold, *Steve Wozniak: A Wizard Called Woz*, p. 59, 65.

[166] Source: Sir Rudolf Bing, *5000 Nights at the Opera*, p. 12.

[167] Source: Ginny Weissman and Coyne Steven Sanders, *The Dick Van Dyke Show*, p. 2.

[168] Source: Robert Gottlieb, *George Balanchine: The Ballet Maker*, p. 14.

[169] Source: Nancy Caldwell Sorel and Edward Sorel, *First Encounters*, p. 51.

[170] Source: Judy Carter, *The Homo Handbook*, p. 186.

[171] Source: Rosalyn M. Story, *And So I Sing: African-American Divas of Opera and Concert*, p. 164.

[172] Source: Leo Slezak, *Song of Motley*, p. 104.

[173] Source: Barrymore Laurence Scherer, *Bravo! A Guide to Opera for the Perplexed*, p. 149.

[174] Source: Robert Tracy and Sharon DeLano, *Balanchine's Ballerinas: Conversations with the Muses*, p. 39.

[175] Source: Wanda Rutkowska, *Famous People in Anecdotes*, p. 34.

[176] Source: Ben Primack, adapter and editor, *The Ben Hecht Show*, pp. 71, 74.

[177] Source: Merlin Holland, *The Wilde Album*, pp. 29-30.

[178] Source: Walter Slezak, *What Time's the Next Swan?*, pp. 210-211.

[179] Source: Eve Arden, *Three Phases of Eve*, p. 58.

[180] Source: H. Allen Smith, *The Compleat Practical Joker*, pp. 61-62.

[181] Source: John Burke, *Rogue's Progress: The Fabulous Adventures of Wilson Mizner*, p. 71.

[182] Source: Redd Foxx and Norma Miller, *The Redd Foxx Encyclopedia of Black Humor*, p. 178.

[183] Source: Paula Bryant Pratt, *Martha Graham*, pp. 65, 67.

[184] Source: Funny Gay Males, *Growing Up Gay*, p. 187.

[185] Source: Eddie Cantor, *As I Remember Them*, pp. 50-51.

[186] Source: Michael Wigge, "5 Ways To Travel The World For Free." Huffington Post. 10 April 2012 <http://www.huffingtonpost.com/michael-wigge/travel-for-free_b_1413200.html>.

[187] Source: Katherine E. Krohn, *Marilyn Monroe: Norma Jeane's Dream*, pp. 51, 74.

[188] Source: Ben Primack, adapter and editor, *The Ben Hecht Show*, p. 32, 195.

[189] Source: Margaret J. Anderson and Karen F. Stevenson, *Scientists of the Ancient World*, pp. 7, 50.

[190] Source: Joe Garner, *Now Showing: Unforgettable Moments from the Movies*, p. 122.

[191] Source: Diane Hodges, *Laugh Lines for Educators*, p. 64.

[192] Source: Alan Wagner, *Prima Donnas and Other Wild Beasts*, pp. 54-55.

[193] Source: Ben Hecht, *Charlie: The Improbable Life and Times of Charles MacArthur*, p. 188.

[194] Source: John Rankin Towse, *Sixty Years of the Theater: An Old Critic's Memories*, pp. 255-256.

[195] Source: Mary Northrup, *American Computer Pioneers*, pp. 32, 36.

[196] Source: Adam Sykes and Iain Sproat, compilers, *The Wit of Westminster*, pp. 18-19.

[197] Source: Gyles Brandreth, *Great Theatrical Disasters*, p. 71.

[198] Source: Betsy Borns, *Comic Lives*, p. 139.

[199] Source: Adam Woog, *Magicians and Illusionists*, p. 49.

[200] Source: Michèle Brown and Ann O'Connor, *Hammer and Tongues*, p. 58.

[201] Source: Jack Goodman and Albert Rice, *I Wish I'd Said That!*, pp. 67-68.

[202] Source: Ted Shawn, *One Thousand and One Night Stands*, p. 198.

[203] Source: Nathan Aaseng, *American Dinosaur Hunters*, pp. 88-89.

[204] Source: Kenneth Williams, *Acid Drops*, pp. 77-78.

[205] Source: Alexei D. Voskressenski, compiler and editor, *Cranks, Knaves, and Jokers of the Celestial*, p. 25.

[206] Source: Rebecca L. Johnson, *Science on the Ice: An Antarctic Journal*, pp. 48, 70-71, 96-97, 100, 102.

[207] Source: Lisa Yount, *Antoine Lavoisier: Founder of Modern Chemistry*, pp. 59-63.

[208] Source: J. Edward Evans, *Charles Darwin: Revolutionary Biologist*, pp. 29, 47-48, 51.

[209] Source: Mary Northrup, *American Computer Pioneers*, pp. 21, 23, 26.

[210] Source: Nathan Aaseng, *American Dinosaur Hunters*, pp. 10, 15.

[211] Source: Carole Ann Camp, *American Astronomers: Searchers and Wanderers*, p. 85.

[212] Source: Claudia de la Roca, "Matt Groening Reveals the Location of the Real Springfield." *Smithsonian Magazine.* May 2012 <http://www.smithsonianmag.com/arts-culture/Matt-Groening-Reveals-the-Location-of-the-Real-Springfield.html>.

[213] Source: Tim Boxer, *The Jewish Celebrity Hall of Fame*, pp. 203-204.

[214] Source: Kermit Schafer, *Best of Bloopers*, pp. 25, 88.

[215] Source: Kermit Schafer, *The Bedside Book of Celebrity Bloopers*, p. 51.

[216] Source: Stanley Holloway, *Wiv a Little Bit O' Luck*, pp. 82-83.

[217] Source: Angelica Shirley Carpenter and Jean Shirley, *L. Frank Baum: Royal Historian of Oz*, pp. 20, 60, 64.

[218] Source: Eve Arden, *Three Phases of Eve*, p. 128.

[219] Source: Nathaniel Benchley, *Robert Benchley*, p. 135.

[220] Source: Dick Richards, compiler, *The Wit of Noël Coward*, p. 38.

[221] Source: Tim Boxer, *The Jewish Celebrity Hall of Fame*, p. 280.

[222] Source: Bill Adler, *Jewish Wit and Wisdom*, p. 50.

[223] Source: Maria Tallchief, *Maria Tallchief: America's Prima Ballerina*, p. 28.

[224] Source: Margaret J. Anderson, *Charles Darwin: Naturalist*, pp. 27, 34, 42.

[225] Source: Merlin Holland, *The Wilde Album*, pp. 16, 101.

[226] Source: Edward Villella, *Prodigal Son: Dancing for Balanchine in a World of Pain and Magic*, p. 185.

[227] Source: Ben Hecht, *Charlie: The Improbable Life and Times of Charles MacArthur*, pp. 14-16.

[228] Source: Michael D. Cole, *John Glenn: Astronaut and Senator*, pp. 28-30, 38, 79.

[229] Source: Corey Ford, *The Time of Laughter*, pp. 113, 129-130.

[230] Source: Leslie Halliwell, *The Filmgoer's Book of Quotes*, pp. 7, 30, 126, 170, 218.

[231] Source: Jim Tully, *A Dozen and One*, pp. 118, 119-120, 122.

[232] Source: Hesketh Pearson, *Lives of the Wits*, pp. 181, 277, 292-293.

[233] Source: Dick Richards, compiler, *The Wit of Peter Ustinov*, pp. 17-18, 55, 107.

[234] Source: Adam Sykes and Iain Sproat, compilers, *The Wit of Westminster*, p. 82.

[235] Source: Kenneth Williams, *Acid Drops*, p. 44.

[236] Source: H. Allen Smith, *Buskin' With H. Allen Smith*, p. 194.

[237] Source: Gyles Brandreth, *Great Theatrical Disasters*, p. 123.

[238] Source: Alexis Petridis, "Jack White: 'I don't like to take the easy way out, on anything I do.'" *Guardian* (UK). 13 April 2012 <http://www.guardian.co.uk/music/2012/apr/13/jack-white-solo-project-blunderbuss>.

[239] Source: John Burke, *Rogue's Progress: The Fabulous Adventures of Wilson Mizner*, pp. 38-39.

[240] Source: Dick Richards, compiler, *The Wit of Peter Ustinov*, pp. 22, 52, 97.

[241] Source: Joan D. Dickinson, *Bill Gates: Billionaire Computer Genius*, pp. 22, 23, 51.

[242] Source: Barbara Kramer, *Amy Tan: Author of* The Joy Luck Club, pp. 33-34.

[243] Source: Bill Crow, *Jazz Anecdotes*, p. vii.

[244] Source: Peter Guttmacher, *Legendary Comedies*, p. 39.

[245] Source: Henry T. Finck, *My Adventures in the Golden Age of Music*, p. 326.

[246] Source: Joe Bob Briggs, *Profoundly Disturbing: Shocking Movies That Changed History!*, p, 102.

[247] Source: Glenhall Taylor, *Before Television*, p. 94.

[248] Source: Joe Bob Briggs, *Profoundly Disturbing: Shocking Movies That Changed History!*, p. 220.

[249] Source: Dick Van Dyke, *Those Funny Kids!*, pp. 31-32.

[250] Source: Joe Franklin, *Joe Franklin's Encyclopedia of Comedians*, p. 103.